Spiritual
Economics

Also by Eric Butterworth

Discover the Power Within You

In the Flow of Life

Unity: A Quest for Truth

Celebrate Yourself!
    And Other Inspirational Essays

Life Is for Living

Life Is for Loving

The Concentric Perspective

MetaMorality: A Metaphysical Approach
    to the Ten Commandments

The Universe Is Calling: Opening to the
    Divine Through Prayer

Spiritual Economics

*The Principles and Process
of True Prosperity*

Eric Butterworth

Unity Village, Missouri

Second revised paperback edition 1998; second printing 2001

Unity House is a publishing imprint of Unity School of Christianity. To receive a catalog of all Unity publications (books, cassettes, compact discs, and magazines) or to place an order, call the Customer Service Department: 816-969-2069 or 1-800-669-0282.

The Revised Standard Version is used for all Bible verses, unless otherwise stated.

Cover design by Gretchen West
Cover photo by © Mark E. Gibson/RO-MA STOCK

Library of Congress Catalog Card Number: 82-50870
ISBN 0-87159-269-X
Canada BN 13252 9033 RT

Library of Congress Cataloging-in-Publication Data
Butterworth, Eric.
    Spiritual economics / Eric Butterworth.
        p.   cm.
    Originally published: 1993.
    ISBN 0-87159-211-8
    1. Wealth—Religious aspects—Unity School of Christianity.
    2. Unity School of Christianity—Doctrines. 3. New Thought.
    I. Title.
    [BX9890.U505B875   1997]
    241'.68—DC21   97-26302
                                                                           CIP

Unity House feels a sacred trust to be a healing presence in the world. By printing with biodegradable soybean ink on recycled paper, we believe we are doing our part to be wise stewards of our Earth's resources.

"What no eye has seen, nor ear heard,
nor the human heart conceived,
what God has prepared for those
who love him."
—*1 Corinthians 2:9 NRSV*

Contents

Foreword to the 1998 Edition

It is impossible to separate the experiences of our life into mutually exclusive categories in such a manner that one does not influence the other or have impact on another. Advancements in science, medicine, art, and indeed economics, all arise from the same source, the creative mind that taps into the inner Self and eventually finds expression in our actions.

The various aspects of our life are all governed by laws that, while not as easy to understand as gravity, are nonetheless as real. In addition, the laws that govern these various aspects are compatible. There is a spiritual aspect to the law that governs human behavior, whether we like it or not.

Eric Butterworth's *Spiritual Economics* puts in clear and concise form the laws that govern economics. These laws are not different because Mr. Butterworth terms them *spiritual* economics. These laws are certain regardless of the label ascribed, and they have not changed in the fifteen years since the book first appeared. You perhaps might be an agnostic. However, the results of allowing your inner thoughts to develop into an expression of action would produce the same results as those of the most devoted student, if the unfolding process were the same. Mr. Butterworth suggests that God does not have a choice, we do.

In the Sermon on the Mount, Jesus tells us that we should go the "second mile," to do *more* than is expected. Is this some pious, abstract, ungrounded truth? Or is this perhaps one of the clearest assertions of economic law? What could be more successful than a retailer that gives more value than is expected?

The life of my employer, Mr. Penney, serves as a wonderful example of spiritual economics in practice as well as spiritual economics aborted. For the first fifteen years of his phenomenally successful retail career, he had a vision that resulted in a retail format that was more efficient, that gave more value and service. He shared that vision, and the success of that vision, with others. His focus was on the process and parallels the steps outlined in Eric Butterworth's *Spiritual Economics*.

The success that Mr. Penney experienced unfortunately led to thoughts, not of service but of self-importance, of power, and yes, of greed. This willingness to succumb to the temptations of personal power had disastrous economic results, apart from the Penney Company.

He found himself both economically and emotionally bankrupt at the age of fifty-seven. Living by spiritual laws had given way to a different voice. However, Mr. Penney, because of his great spiritual foundation, was able to overcome and eventually triumph over this misdirection.

The technological gains of the twentieth century have broken down barriers and have allowed a more free flow of the universal intelligence that is available to all of us. The twenty-first century will no doubt accelerate this process. It is impossible to imagine the great economic gains that come from the expansion of universal Mind through the sharing of knowledge and vision plus the willingness to let all benefit from its collective force.

Within each of us is an inner urge to live life to its fullest, and to share that fullness with others as well. Eric Butterworth has succinctly detailed the steps that are necessary to achieve this fullness. He appropriately warns that it is not the accumulation of "things," but the will to serve and share the abundant life which is available if we are willing to listen to our inner Source and to translate our inner voice into vision and action.

My personal experience confirms the truth of Eric Butterworth's message. Grabbing for the "Gold Ring" without quiet listening and affirmation generally has resulted in financial loss; however, patience and a carefully reasoned desire to serve have produced financial rewards.

Considering the historic view of human progress, we have unimaginable benefits yet to realize as co-creators in shaping the earth's unlimited bounty to the good of all.

David F. Miller
March 1997

David F. Miller is retired vice chairman of the board and chief operating officer of the JC Penney Company, Inc.

Preface

Ours is an age of great change. Great corporations are streamlining their workforce to reflect the need for greater efficiencies of operation and also for the impact of automation. Whole industries are either being eliminated entirely or are moving into new fields. The result: jobs once considered to be secure are being eliminated. Many workers are being faced with the need to undergo retraining for entry into new fields of work. Many people are launching out in entrepreneurial endeavors, calling for faith and vision and the need to tap into the universal flow of substance.

Healthful is a common word which connotes "conducive to health," that is good food, plenty of rest, and an environment of high vibrations. There is no word, however, that relates to the things that make for a personal experience of wealth . . . and there should be. So I have taken the liberty of coining the word *wealthful*. It is a wonderful word. I recommend it to you. Use it often.

There is a great need to establish ourselves in those things that are conducive to prosperity. We need to turn the focus of our attention away from lack, layoffs, and limitations, and on to the omnipresence of universal substance. We can see it in the everywhere presence of life all through nature, and we can feel it in the endless flow of creative ideas that issues forth from our minds in moments of inspiration. Just as there are experiences that are healthful to us, so are there experiences that are "wealthful."

Expose yourself constantly to wealthful ideas—think prosperity, think substance, think affluence. Your life will be influenced for good or ill by the kinds of thoughts that rule your mind and manifest in your world. *Spiritual Economics* is all about such thoughts. I strongly recommend it to you. And supported by the testimony of scores of people who have written to tell of the positive influence on their lives of working with this book, I sincerely believe it can be a wealthful influence in your life.

—*Eric Butterworth*

Introduction

"Greater than the tread of mighty armies is an idea whose time has come."

—*Victor Hugo*

This is a book about true prosperity. The concepts it articulates are applicable to governments and to people. You have been drawn to the book by divine appointment, so it just could be that *Spiritual Economics* is an idea whose time has come in your life.

Can you accept Emerson's dictum that you are born to be rich or inevitably to grow rich by the use of your faculties? If not, perhaps you are hung up on the age-old confusion of godliness with poverty. Lack and limitation of any kind are aberrations in an opulent Universe. Any person who is experiencing lack is, in some way, living in opposition to the universal flow.

Charles Fillmore, co-founder of Unity School of Christianity, shocked the religious establishment of his day (and ours) when he said, "It is a sin to be poor!" He wasn't referring to moral turpitude, but rather to "the frustration of potentiality." He believed and taught that, when we establish ourselves in the consciousness of God, the whole Universe moves to flow into us with its abundance of life and substance. This is obviously what Jesus had in mind when he said, "But seek first his kingdom and his righteousness, and all these things shall be yours as well" (Mt. 6:33).

It has been commonly assumed that in times of economic reverses, we are all victims of a strange malaise about which there is little that can be done other than to wait and see. However, the study of the laws of spiritual economics reveals that there is much we can do, personally for ourselves, and in concert for our country and our world.

The belief is all too common that financial limitation is simply a quirk of bad luck ("I have been down on my luck lately") or the result of the capricious will of God. So, ordinary people may hope for better things, and they may even try to change their luck by playing the lottery. They may also fantasize about happy and abundant living. But they will make little or no attempt to be other than what they believe themselves to be—and financial limitation is part of what they believe themselves to be.

Even as most physical ills are now considered to be psychosomatic in origin, so we must begin to face the possibility that financial problems may be the outer manifestation of inner states of consciousness. A great idea whose time has come is that there is no such thing as a purely financial problem unrelated to false attitudes and emotions which caused it or a healthy attitude or emotion which can cure it.

To get the most from this study, you will want to declare your independence from the belief that your personal welfare is completely tied to the economic fluctuations of the world "out there." You will also want to establish yourself in the unassailable conviction that the free flow of substance can only be dammed up from within and that no one can keep your good from you but you. As you become conscious of the laws of spiritual economics, you can effect some really dramatic life changes "from indigence to affluence."

The word *affluence* is an overworked word in our time, usually implying cars and houses and baubles of all kinds. Its literal meaning is "an abundant flow," and not things at all. When we are consciously centered in the universal flow, we experience inner direction and the unfoldment of creative activity. Things come too, but prosperity is not just having things. It is the consciousness that attracts things.

Let me make it clear at the outset that I am in complete disagreement with the growing emphasis in the metaphysical movement on money and things as objects of the study and practice of Truth. I agree with John Ruskin who said, "What right have you to take the word *wealth*, which originally meant 'well-being,' and degrade and narrow it by confining it to certain sorts of material objects measured by money."

The word *prosperity* has been corrupted to imply gold dust falling from the sky. The word *millionaire* is overworked to appeal to the student's acquisitive instinct. And dollar signs often adorn the covers of prosperity books to suggest that the amassing of wealth is a kind of spiritual growth. I look upon all this as gross materialization of a beautiful spiritual Truth.

The word *prosperity* comes from the Latin root which literally translates: "according to hope" or "to go forward hopefully." Thus it is not so much a condition in life as it is an attitude toward life. The truly prosperous person is what psychologist Rollo May calls "the fully functioning person," one who is experiencing what Jesus called the life more abundant. I say:

> Prosperity is a way of living and thinking,
> and not just money or things.
> Poverty is a way of living and thinking,
> and not just a lack of money or things.

Considered in the broadest sense, prosperity is "spiritual well-being." This involves the whole experience of healing life, satisfying love, abiding peace and harmony as well as a sufficiency of what Aristotle called the "furniture of fortune." Too often the tendency is for teacher and student to become so preoccupied with the demonstration of jobs and bank accounts as to forget that the person is a whole creature in a whole Universe. While in this work, we are focusing on spiritual economics, we are forever conscious of a backdrop of spiritual ecology, the Truth that sets us free from all the problems of human experience. It is consciousness that sets all the limits in life, if there are any limits. We have been erroneously conditioned to believe that our lives are completely shaped by what happens around us and to us. But life is lived from within-out. It is not what happens "out there," but what we do or think about what happens.

The starting point in realizing prosperity is to accept responsibility for your own thoughts, thus taking charge of your life. You are not responsible for what is said in the *Wall Street Journal* or what comes out of Washington in the form of economic indicators, but you are very much responsible for what you *think* about these things. You cannot afford to let the so-called experts decide how you are going to think and feel. For how you think and feel about the economy in general and your financial affairs in particular will unvaryingly determine what you experience.

If you are serious about the program suggested by this book, you will want to make a commitment to get yourself and keep yourself in the positive stream of life. Refuse to indulge in casual conversation (should the word be *causal*?) about the bad economy, the high cost of living, or about anything you really do not want to say "yes" to. Eliminate such thoughts as "I can't," "I'm afraid," and

"There is not enough" from your consciousness. Talk only about the things you want to see live and grow. Keep your thoughts centered in the ideas of abundance, sufficiency, and well-being. And occasionally give yourself a consciousness booster by affirming something like:

God is my instant, constant, and abundant source of supply.

In a regular meditation practice, work on the realization that you are surrounded by a divine Presence which wishes for you only good because you are expressing its life. The biting truth is that God will make you prosperous and successful in all your ways if you do not make it too hard for God. Infinite Mind will put ideas into your mind, words into your mouth, creativity into your hands, boundless opportunity before you, and guiding light on your way.

All that is required is that you keep yourself centered in the creative flow, keep in tune through positive thoughts, keep responsive by your faith, and as Thoreau would say, "Keep moving in the direction of your dreams."

Let me remind you again that this book is a program for personal practice and discipline. Avoid the temptation to stop short with the reading. All too many students are over-read and under-done. Our goal is to help you develop a rich mentality that will be impervious to the fluctuations of the economy. More than this, we want to become, collectively, a positive influence toward stabilizing those fluctuations.

CHAPTER 1

The Truth About Substance

Most of us have grown up under the influence of religions that dealt with a Universe of many parts: God and heaven above, Earth and human life beneath, hell and Satan under the Earth. Perhaps we have been freed from the latter, and we may have come to an "omni" view of the former. But too often we have failed to get it all together. This is what religion should be. The word *religion* comes from a root word that means "bind together." Thus the word actually means unity, oneness, wholeness.

Unfortunately, religions have been institutions instead of perceptions, something you join rather than a transcendence you experience. We have been conditioned to believe that God works exclusively through the machinery of an ecclesiastical body. We need to refresh ourselves with the vision of Paul's sermon on Mars Hill:

> "The God who made the world and everything in it, being Lord of heaven and earth, does not live in shrines made by man, nor is he served by human hands, as though he needed anything, since he himself gives to all men life and breath and every-thing. . . . Yet he is not far from each one of us, for 'In him we live and move and have our being.'"
>
> *Acts 17:24–25, 27–28*

When you think of God, you may follow the subcon-scious tendency to think *up* to a giant Michelangelo-like figure of a superman, with bulging muscles and a long white beard, sitting alone on his billowy cloud throne, with all the wealth of the Universe "in His hands." You may insist that you do not hold such an image. Perhaps not. But when you pray for God's help in some financial problem, do you ask God for supply from God's all-sufficiency?

H. Emilie Cady, the New Thought pioneer and author of the influential *Lessons in Truth*, poses a challenging in-sight that every sincere seeker after Truth should reflect upon: "God is not a being with qualities or attributes, but He is the good itself coming into expression as life, love, power, wisdom." What this says is that God is not loving, God is the allness of love. God is not wise, God is the allness of wisdom. God is not a dispenser of divine substance, God is the allness of ever-present substance in which we live, move, and have being. And this is the subtle but vitally important key on which the entire structure of spiritual economics rests.

The word *substance* comes from the Latin "substare," which means "stand under." There is a substance standing under everything. We are not referring just to the component parts that make up the thing, but to the nonmaterial essence at the root of it. Today we know much about molecules and atoms and subatomic particles. But what is not commonly known is that the focus of research is now being centered, not on the minute particles of the material, but on what is called "the reality of the nonmaterial." The space between them is now considered more important than the particles themselves. In this space is to be found a field of force that holds the particles in their orbits. It is even being conjectured that the particle is not just acted upon by the force, but it is the force acting as a particle. Certainly this has application in our relation to God: We are not just acted upon by God, but *we are* the activity of God expressing as us.

We talk of faith that God will provide, but what do we mean? We will be dealing with faith in a later chapter. But for now, let us be clear on one thing: Faith doesn't influence God "out there" to send riches to fill our needs "down here." Faith is the spiritual capacity by which we may form and shape this ever-present basic element of

Spirit-substance. Mike Todd once put this awareness in the simplest way when he said, "Many times I have been broke, but I have never been poor." Any person who understands this will have in his or her possession the key by which he or she will always be able to demonstrate prosperity and security no matter what the conditions in the world.

Jesus said, "In the world you have tribulation; but . . . I have overcome the world" (Jn. 16:33). It would appear that he was saying that he had achieved access to heaven which gave him a divine dispensation on Earth. Not so! He was implying that we live in two realms, not in succession, but concurrently. In other words, we live in the world of tribulation, where we experience health and sickness, abundance and lack, joy and sadness. But at the same time we also live in the Universe, the realm of the constancy and stability of a basic substance that stands beneath every human experience. Thus it can be said (and should be) that there is an Allness within every illness, an All-Sufficiency within every appearance of lack, and the "joy of the Lord" within every moment of sorrow.

So, when Jesus said, "I have overcome the world," he meant that he kept himself centered in the inner realm of wholeness. He knew that he might experience less, but he could never be less than a dynamic center in a whole Universe. And the thing which makes Jesus' teaching so powerfully relevant to contemporary times is his insistence that all that he did we can do too, if we have faith. In other words, if we keep ourselves centered in that inner realm of wholeness, as he so persistently did, we, too, can experience mastery over all that happens around us or to us. The centering process is the key to achieving prosperity.

When we use the word *Universe*, we are not just referring to the vast cosmos of galaxies out there, for all that is simply the accumulation of an infinite number of other worlds. No, we are using the word in a more transcendent sense. The word *Universe*, in its literal meaning, is "the whole body of things," the basic unity of all life. Actually, we are implying a larger thought of God. The words *God* and *Universe* can be used interchangeably, referring to the whole of things, or Allness, which is present in all and through all.

In the universal realm, in which you live and have being, the whole of God is present at every point in space at the same time. This is a fantastic concept. Read those words again: *The whole of God is present at every point in space at the same time.* Take time to meditate on this great idea. In other words, God doesn't come and go. God doesn't capriciously move substance from God's supply "up there" to fill your need "down here." Nor does God answer prayer in some special kind of coming forth. God is always present, totally present—as a Presence. You may be praying for healing, but the Truth is, the whole of God-life is present as a healing Presence. When you know this, you are beginning to understand what spiritual healing is all about. You may be praying for increased supply, but the whole of God-substance is present as a prospering Presence. Know this and you are on the way to achieving prosperity. This concept may challenge you to rethink the whole practice of prayer and to appreciate the simple logic of the Psalmist who said: "Be still, and know that I am God" (Ps. 46:10).

Be sure to catch the implication of this great Truth as it concerns God as substance: The whole of God-substance is present in its entirety at every point in space at the same time. Not just *some* of it, but *all* the substance in the Universe is present at any point of human need. Someone has said, "There is no spot where God is not." There is no place on Earth where there is an absence of substance.

Now, while there is no limitation, there may be a consciousness of limitation. Thus there may be many "pockets of poverty" in the world and countless victims of deprivation. However, the Truth is, despite the appearance of great lack, in every area, in every human life, "there is an infinite and eternal energy from which all things proceed." You may be far from knowing this at times. Like Mike Todd, you might even be "broke." But the Allness of substance is present where you are, so you shouldn't be poor.

There is no place in all the Universe where substance is any more present or any less present than right where you are. Could there be a point on Earth where gravity has any more pull or any less pull than the point where you are? And also, though you can accumulate and store away material riches, there is no way that you can amass substance. In contrast to this, you could lose all your assets in a financial crisis, but you can never lack substance. The awareness of this principle marked the difference in the crash of 1929 between those who picked themselves up and went on and those who jumped out of windows. A person who keeps conscious that the divine flow is ever centered within one has faith that limitless substance will find expression through him or her in the form of creative ideas, ingenuity, the will to work, and a security of work opportunities. It could be said that when you realize your relationship to the dynamic Universe, you are forever in a field where you can drill for oil and bring in a gusher every time.

In the immortal Sermon on the Mount, Jesus said:

> "Do not lay up for yourselves treasures on earth, where moth and rust consume and where thieves break in and steal, but lay up for yourselves treasures in heaven, where neither moth nor rust consumes and where thieves do not break in and steal. For where your treasure is, there will your heart be also."
>
> ***Matthew 6:19–21***

He was talking about the focus of our consciousness, not just what we do, but what we think and feel, how we visualize our relationship with things. Many are the heartaches of the person who bases his or her whole security on things of the world. Inflation, recessions, and high costs are among the many moths and rusts that consume and the thieves that break through and steal. Peaceful and secure is the person whose real treasure is always the affluence of God-substance. He or she always feels rich no matter how the market fluctuates or what the balance sheet shows. And the great thing is that this feeling will prompt him or her always to make right and wise decisions in the management of his or her affairs. The mind flourishes with creative ideas, the hands tingle with ingenuity, opportunities unfold, and blessings abound—all because of the feeling of abundance that came first.

Get it into your consciousness that you live in substance as a fish lives in water. It is basically your milieu. Can the fish of the sea ever lack for water? Can you, having your being in the sea of God-substance, ever really lack for a sufficiency of creativity or ideas or money or opportunities in any time of need? The important thing is to hold to the awareness that you are created in substance, formed of substance, and ceaselessly supported by substance. Paraphrasing Emerson, the free flow of substance in your life is the continuation of the divine effort that made you in the first place.

You may be thinking that when you have a financial problem that it seems perfectly natural to go out into the world to raise the money. Of course, when there are bills to be paid and needs to be met there are things to do. As the Quakers say, "When you pray, move your feet." Do what you can do with what you have. Apply yourself a little more diligently in your work or in your effort to find work. Make your needs known to your employer or to other selected agencies as and if you are guided. Of course, "God helps those who help themselves." However, there is a greater Truth: God can do no more *for* you than God can do *through* you. All the help of God cannot aid you except as it flows through your consciousness, through your faith, through your vision. So before you attempt to raise money, the first step should be to raise consciousness, to know that "the place on which you are standing is holy ground" (Ex. 3:5). It is important to recall that it is not really for lack of abundance that you are experiencing want, but for lack of the awareness of the ever-present reality of divine substance and the faith to shape it into manifest form.

Turn from the appearance of lack to the reality of affluence as you declare for yourself something like this: *I establish myself in the limitless substance of God, and I have abundance.*

It is a profound realization. But remember, these words do not become true because you affirm them. This is the common confusion about the practice of affirmative prayer, that if you speak words of Truth over and over, you impress them on the subconscious mind and thus they become true for you. They do not become true because you affirm them. You affirm them because they are true. You are synchronizing your consciousness with the reality of Truth, creating a channel through which the mystical flow may do its powerful work through you.

The exciting thing about omnipresent substance is that it is so abundant that no one need ever have less in order that you may have more. In the world of business, there may be a mad scramble for the world's plums. There is a tendency to get caught up in the idea of competition in the struggle of trying to get ahead of other people while fearing that they will get ahead of you. But in the spiritual realm, there can be no competition, nor the need for it. People have their own pipelines to the universal good, and if they are true to themselves and keep centered in God-consciousness, their own will surely come without strain or struggle. When you breathe all the air you need, you can never deprive anyone else of all the air each person needs to breathe. There is always enough with plenty to spare because all the substance is present in its entirety at every point. Thus, if you sense that another person is straining to get ahead of you, be sure you do not lower yourself to that person's fear vibration. Affirm for him or her: *I bless you with the awareness that you are one with your own personal flow of the Universe in which there is a legitimate royal abundance for every living creature.*

In the Truth about substance, it is imperative that every person gets the realization of *entitlement*. Jesus made a special point of this when he said emphatically, "Come, O blessed of my Father, inherit the kingdom prepared for you

from the foundation of the world" (Mt. 25:34). You are entitled to it; you have inherited it; it is yours. The foundation of the world is the fundamental realm of spiritual law
of the Universe in which you live. The kingdom is that
within you which is your very own inlet that may become
an outlet to all there is in God. Claim your inheritance
of abundance. You are entitled to the support of God-
substance in everything to which you give your mind or
hands. Let go of the old belief in the "grace" of poverty
and the subconscious sense of guilt in having things,
along with feelings of unworthiness—attitudes that have
such a detrimental influence upon human consciousness.
Claim your entitlement. *I am a child of the Universe,
richly endowed with the fullness of All-Good.* A child of the
Universe! Can you get that into your consciousness? Not
just the offspring of your parents or a product of the
times, but a child of the Universe. You are an expression
of the infinite creative flow, entitled to as constant support
as the lilies of the field.

You see, the basis of entitlement is the startling asser-
tion: The Universe owes you a living! Yes, we are saying
owes you a living. Note: We are not saying that the *world*
owes you a living. Actually, the world owes you nothing.
You are a creative expression of the Universe, with the
responsibility to let your light shine. Thus you owe the
world a life. But in all the many ways in which you apply
yourself in the world, the Universe owes you complete
support.

The confusion of our social welfare system comes from the democratic ideal that the world owes everyone an opportunity for secure living. When this is not understood, how easily it gives rise to the "welfare state" of universal dependency on the government. Now, certainly, out of love and compassion, a civilized society may want to ensure that every person has a subsistency, which is good. But in the world, no one should be "entitled" to support. Each of us is an individualized expression of the creative process, no matter how circumstances have obscured the reality. The great need is to help us to know this for ourselves, to claim our own "entitlement" from within. When persons in poverty begin to know, really know, that they are a center within an affluent Universe, then in ways of personal motivation, ingenuity, guidance, and the unfoldment of opportunities, the whole Universe will soon be rushing, streaming, pouring into them from all sides.

The glorious Truth is that you are a very special person, and you always have something special working within you, flowing through you. The whole Universe is on your side. Life is forever biased on the side of healing, on the side of overcoming, on the side of success. When you get yourself centered in the universal flow, you become synchronized with this divine bias for good. Amazing things can and will unfold. Some will call them miracles, but you will accept them as the perfectly natural function of the divine process.

This process is beautifully symbolized in the Old Testament story of the widow who came to the prophet Elisha in distress (2 Kings 4:1–7). She had been left destitute by the death of her husband. Her creditors were pressing her, and her two sons, according to Talmudic law, were forfeit for her debt. She cried out to Elisha, saying in effect, "My husband is dead, and the creditor has come to take my sons." Elisha asked, "What have you in the house?" She replied, "I have only one pot of oil!" You see, what he was asking her was, "Where is your consciousness? What are you thinking about? What are you identifying with?" Her reply indicated that, despite the one pot of oil, she was centered in the awareness of poverty. She was possessed by fear and thus had cut herself off from the divine flow. She had a pot of oil, but to her, it was *only* one pot. It was evidence of substance, but to her, it was a symbol of lack. She was plagued with the very common problem of "onliness."

How much money do you earn in your job? What is your net worth? In most cases, you would respond, "I only earn . . ." "I am only worth . . ." Why the "only"? In other words, regardless of what you have, your thoughts are subtly centered in what you do not have, with the subconscious fear that you do not have enough. It is said of Jesus that he went forth without scrip or purse. He didn't have anything in terms of assets, but he had faith. He had the awareness of the whole of God-substance present wherever he might be. It may not be necessary for you to go forth without money in your pocket or in the bank. And in our day it may be unwise to do so. But you do need to walk and work from the same level of consciousness as that expressed by Jesus, the same feeling of affluence, the same attunement to the creative flow. Whatever you have in the house, let it not be identified with an "only." Let what you have in your job, your possessions, your resources be the symbol of the presence of limitless substance. To the extent that you can do this, the job will prosper and the assets will increase. Jesus put it very simply, "But seek first his kingdom and his righteousness, and all these things shall be yours as well" (Mt. 6:33).

Now, Elisha instructed the widow to go to her neighbors and borrow additional vessels. This suggests the need to expand the mind to include new faith and vision, to try on some new insights for size. She did borrow additional vessels, which meant she broadened her horizon of expectations. She poured the oil from her one pot into the new vessels, and it flowed freely till the last vessel was filled. When there were no more vessels, the oil stopped. In other words, as much as she could conceive and believe, she could achieve.

Paul says, "My God will supply every need of yours according to his riches" (Phil. 4:19). God is a ceaseless flow of substance, and no matter what the extent of the need, universal substance can easily supply it. But there is one thing God cannot do. God cannot supply lack. This is because lack is a state of mind, and the condition cannot be remedied until the state of mind is altered. The one jar of oil to the widow was her lack, due to her feeling of "onliness." However, when she expanded her faith through providing additional vessels, the lack became a legitimate need, which was instantly and abundantly filled.

If you have a financial problem, perhaps a great need for increased prosperity, "What do you have in the house?" Where is your consciousness? Borrow additional vessels, which means, raise your consciousness, widen your horizon of faith. Identify yourself with the idea that you are entitled to the boundless support of the Universe. Really believe this. It could be that by careful study of the ideas of this book, you are effectively "adding vessels" and expanding your vision of entitlement to God-substance.

But remember, you do not have to *get* more substance, for all the substance of the Universe is present right where you are. It may be very human to want to set a goal for yourself during the study of this book to acquire certain sums of money or a better job or a new apartment or house. But, you see, in terms of substance, that which stands under, all of it is present right now. We are talking about the creative flow, the new ideas, the inward spiritual power by which you can do all that you want or need to do. Watch your spiritual priorities. The goal should not be to make money or acquire things, but to achieve the consciousness through which the substance will flow forth when and as you need it.

In this book, we will discuss many facets of the prosperity "gem," but you might as well know at the outset that _there is only one way by which you can achieve prosperity_. It is to take charge of your mind. You may be looking for some magic formula, some new metaphysical cliché that will change things. But if you want to change your life, you will have to alter your thoughts. The whole of infinite substance is present where you are, but you will have to get that awareness into your consciousness by your own discipline and commitment. So if you find yourself responding to life's question, "What have you in the house?" with a plethora of "onlys," cut right into that flow of negativity and affirm:

I am a richly endowed expression of an opulent Universe. There is always a sufficiency to do the things I want and need to do.

In her classic work _Lessons in Truth_, H. Emilie Cady says:

> One of the unerring Truths in the Universe is that there is already provided a lavish abundance for every human want. In other words, the supply of every good always awaits the demand. Another Truth is that the demand must be made before the supply can come forth to fill it.

In other words, we must provide the vessels in which the oil may be increased. There must be a need before we attract an answer. And Jesus indicated that there must be an asking before there can be a receiving. This certainly does not suggest that we should start pleading with the skies for help. It has been a very confused point in traditional Christianity, which has considered the asking as supplicating a capricious God. It is interesting that the word *ask* as Jesus uses it comes from the Greek root which has a strong connotation toward "claim or demand."

You ask for water from the faucet by turning the tap. You ask for light from the lamp by throwing the switch. You ask gravity to hold you in your seat by sitting erect and balanced. Jesus said, "It is your Father's good pleasure to give you the kingdom" (Lk. 12:32). That certainly does not sound as if he expected us to engage in special appeals. He even said, "Your Father knows what you need before you ask him" (Mt. 6:8). Then why need we ask at all? It is obvious that, to God, asking was simply a claim of entitlement, a receptivity of consciousness. It is creating the condition in mind that makes the result inevitable.

In the ensuing chapters, we will deal with many of the ways in which we may "ask" God for supply, by creating the consciousness through which the limitlessness of universal substance may flow. This calls to mind the wisdom of Lao-tzu who, 2500 years ago, proved that there is nothing new in New Thought:

The human spirit has its source in the divine fountain which must be permitted to flow freely through man. Anyone who flows as life flows has solved the enigma of human existence and needs no other power. Anything is evil that blocks the flow of creative action, and everything is healthy (prosperous) that flows with the Universe.

The medieval mystic lay monk Brother Lawrence coined the illumining phrase, "The practice of the presence of God." This is often erroneously thought of as a somber act of religious piety. In the context of Brother Lawrence's experience of working for God while scrubbing pots in the monastery kitchen, it doesn't seem to mean having flashes of mystical insight or even spending long periods in meditation. It is said of doctors that they "practice medicine." That certainly does not suggest having an emotional experience. It is purely a description of how they make their living.

To practice the presence of God does not mean to titillate yourself with some mysterious spirit of God that comes and goes. The Presence of God is that of God which is *present*, wholly present, ceaselessly present. It never changes. It doesn't come and go. It is! You may change, and like the Prodigal Son, you may come and go. But as Meister Eckhart says, "You are in the far country, the Father is at home." So the practice of the Presence means continually reminding yourself of the activity of God ever working in you, much as the student of mathematics must continually remind himself or herself of the principles.

Make a deeply rooted commitment that you will practice the Presence of God-substance, ever reminding yourself that you are in the Presence of an infinite, eternal substance from which all things proceed. Resolve that you will live and think and work as if you really believed that the whole Universe of creativity and substance were present in every project of your work and every transaction of your investments as your never-failing resource.

Practice the presence of God-substance with diligence and persistence, and you will begin to realize prosperity.

CHAPTER 2

Your Fortune Begins With You

The study of what we call "The New Insight in Truth" is for many persons an extremely intriguing experience, but it really does not begin to make much sense or to enable you to make changes in your life until you accept the law of consciousness.

It may be that one of the great moments in the long evolution of man on planet Earth was when some primitive "Alley-Oop" first got an inkling that he could be free, that he could have some control over his destiny. It didn't mean, nor did he think it did, that he could control the elements or the giant beasts which roamed his world. However, it did mean that he could take charge of his own life and do certain things of his own volition which would determine the influence of outer conditions and creatures upon his life. It was one of the great moments in human history.

And it is an important moment in your life when you discover for yourself the great Truth that things may happen around you, and things may happen to you, but the only things which really count are the things that happen in you. You may have precious little control of the elements or the fluctuation of the stock market or the unpredictable behavior of people. However, you live in a world of your consciousness, which is the sum total of the thoughts of your mind. And you can control what goes on in your mind. This is not to say that it is easy but to establish that it is possible. There is a great idea that you will encounter again and again on your quest: you are a living magnet, constantly drawing to you the things, the people, and the circumstances which are in accord with your thoughts. In other words, you are where you are in experience, in relationships, even in financial conditions, because of what you are (which is where you are in consciousness). Now, this is not an easy teaching. You may want to reject it and put the book aside. In the Bible, when Jesus began to lay out the hard laws of his teaching, it says, "Many of his disciples drew back and no longer went about with him" (Jn. 6:66). And thus it has always been. However, if you are willing to accept full responsibility for your life, then even as your level of thought has put you where you are (or at least contributed to it), so by a change of consciousness, you can change the experiences of your life.

This would seem not to apply in the case of the nation's economy and its influence on your personal prosperity. Certainly there are broad differences of opinion among the world's economists. However, we can be certain of one thing: by reason of the law of sequence and consequence, every cycle had to start somewhere. It is likely that someone or some group of persons set forth a strongly felt belief which spread like fire and swept across the country, having a measurable influence upon consumer buying, the job market, the inflationary spiral, and on the performance of the stock market. One thing which economists do agree upon is that business conditions always tend to reflect the level of confidence of the people.

On a more personal level, your own prosperity or lack of it will also reflect the level of your thinking. There is just no way around it: your fortune (good or bad) begins with you. Financial crises, even recessions or depressions, so far as they affect your pocketbook or bank account or job stability, begin with your reactions of faith or fear. You do not cause economic conditions, though we all share in the cumulative consciousness that is the cause; but if you give them reality by your negative thoughts or conversations about them, you become synchronized with an energy flow which has as swift an influence on your life as the light that bathes the room when you throw the switch. You do not make the light, but in a very real sense, it becomes real in your experience by reason of your act of turning it on. Someone could say, "You are fortunate to have light in your room." But your fortune begins with you.

Your personal welfare begins with your consciousness. It is not what happens on Wall Street. It is not the "state of the economy." It has its inception in the state of your mind. You can be prosperous when business is poor, and you can experience financial difficulties even when business is booming.

Consider, if you will, the responsibility you have toward conditions as a whole. For what happens in your mind and is reflected in your affairs will have a definite, even if minuscule, influence upon the nation's business. There is no way out: you are always on the side of the problem, or you are on the side of the solution. "Choose this day whom you will serve" (Josh. 24:15).

However, as concerns prosperity for you, it is simply a matter of addition or subtraction. By your thinking, you are either adding to your good or you are taking away from it. The law is inexorable. Failure or lack in your life is simply the result of continuously "minus-ing" yourself. Conversely, success and prosperity are the results of constantly "plus-ing" yourself. It is wise to take inventory occasionally. Are you dealing in minuses or pluses? It is that simple. Your negative thoughts of fear and worry are depleting your good faster than inflation erodes the value of the dollar. And your positive, optimistic thoughts add to your good more dramatically than compound interest increases your bank savings.

Jesus declared this Truth in a statement that has been extremely controversial. He said, "For unto every one that hath shall be given, and he shall have abundance: but from him that hath not shall be taken away even that which he hath" (Mt. 25:29 KJV). To many persons, this seems to say that the rich get richer and the poor get poorer, which certainly would appear to be a great injustice. Actually, Jesus' statement puts into symbolical language the kind of orderly law upon which the whole Universe is constructed.

Remember that little horseshoe-shaped piece of steel painted red which we played with as children? We would use it to pick up metallic objects and to find things in the sand. A magnet attracts and holds iron filings. Yet if you take an unmagnetized piece of steel, even if it is shaped like a horseshoe and painted red, it not only attracts no filings, but even if you heap some filings on the steel, they will fall off at the first jostling. This is not favoritism or luck. It is basic universal law. Thus in the same sense you are constantly attracting to you the conditions you make inevitable by the quality of your thoughts.

In the teaching of Truth, there is a lot of emphasis given to "making demonstrations." The student may say "I am trying to demonstrate over this . . ." or "I'm working to demonstrate a new job . . ." It is a term used in *scientific prayer*, the concept that if you get certain things worked out within your consciousness, you are going to "outform" or manifest them in your experience. Answered prayer, then, is a "demonstration." In the science of prayer, nothing is incurable or beyond help; all things are possible. It is a tremendously important realization. However, in the minds of many students, it is a matter of making divine law work. You can't make law work. Law is an inexorable process. You are always in the working milieu of law, as, for example, you are always under the influence of gravity. One might be foolish to say, "I am going to make a demonstration of gravity." The fact is gravity is a constant. You may stray from the awareness of the process and do some unwise thing that will revert to you as a problem. If so, the need is simply to stop doing it and once again become synchronized with gravity's supportive vibration. So it is with the demonstration of divine law. It is not something you do to God or even something that God does especially for you. It is simply a change of your consciousness in which you become synchronized with the ceaseless activity of divine love, of healing life, or of prospering substance.

In the metaphysical teaching of prosperity, the idea of demonstration, unfortunately, is often presented in terms of magic and miracles. We hear things like "the magic of demonstration" and the "miracle of answered prayer." There is the suggestion of alchemy, turning things into something else or producing something "ex nihilo," out of nothing. You may recall the wilderness story of Jesus, when he was tempted by the devil to turn stones into bread or change spiritual awareness into worldly power.

Don't miss the meaning here by imagining an outside tempter luring him on. The devil is the satanic influence of human consciousness, urging him to try to find short-cuts to personal fortune. Jesus held firm in self-realization and self-control as he said, "Get thee hence, Satan" (Mt. 4:10 KJV).

The important Truth is that you are a spiritual being with the Allness of Infinite Mind within you. Whatever your needs may be, the answer is not to get God to give you more through some divine sleight-of-hand process, but rather to uncover and release your own "imprisoned splendor." Avoid the temptation to try to "work the law" and thus to materialize the process. Get your mind off the idea of making a demonstration *in* life. Center your awareness on a deeper sense of life, and the demonstration will begin to make you.

Well-intentioned enthusiasts of New Thought often echo the misleading cliché, "Expect a miracle!" It is supposed to encourage one to expect more from life, which is good. However, it is walking right into a trap. So I say, against the grain of the majority of most contemporary teachings and teachers of Truth, *"Don't expect a miracle!"* If you center your consciousness in the expectation of miracles, you are playing with universal law, hoping for some magic abrogation of its inexorable activity. You are putting the whole weight of your consciousness on the side of belief in a Universe of caprice. It is spiritual naïveté, which dilutes all that you may have built up in the awareness of the changelessness of divine law.

This is certainly not to express skepticism of the tremendous power to heal or prosper or to question in any way the full implications of the statement, "All things are possible." When we deal with changeless law, we have even more faith in the process, but we don't have to play games. When the widow's oil was increased, it was not through divine intervention in human affairs, but the exploitation of divine law on a higher level of awareness. Certainly all things are possible, not because God makes an exception for you by reason of your plea, but because your faith is the key to the kingdom of the power within you to apply the laws that transcend human limitation.

Again we say, don't expect a miracle! Don't reduce the practice of Truth to the naive effort to coax a magic showing from a reticent God. If you really believe that you are "entitled" to the fullness of the kingdom, the resulting "outforming" may *appear* to be miraculous, for wonderful things can and will be done, but it is the natural fulfillment of divine law. The healing you long for, the overcoming you desire, the prosperity and success you have been praying for so persistently—even though you may feel there are fantastic odds to overcome—these things do not call for miracles but for the disciplined application of divine law and the steady effort to know God.

The great ideal of spiritual seeking is to be "in tune with the Infinite." To traffic in such thoughts as "Only a miracle can save him," and "It is impossible, but I expect a miracle" is to be in tune with the indefinite. Think about this. Get it clearly established in consciousness. There are no miracles in an orderly Universe. All things are possible under divine law.

One of the most self-limiting attitudes of the whole human race is the belief in chance or luck. Occasionally it is said, "I have been lucky; my prayer was answered." However, God doesn't deal in luck. As Emerson says, "The dice of God are always loaded." The belief in luck crowds out real faith and lulls all true initiative to sleep. And yet so many people think that prosperity and success are simply the results of good luck and that financial reverses, unemployment, even illnesses are "misfortunes" or bad luck. It is the most flourishing excuse for all human difficulties. It soothes the conscience and presents the person as an innocent victim of an unknown, sinister force. We say, in an almost pious declaration of self-defense, "I couldn't do much about it; I was just unlucky."

It is often in this consciousness of spiritual immaturity that a person may turn to "the wheel of fortune" as a way to strike it rich. A person may have an urgent financial need and think, I will make my demonstration by picking the winning number in the lottery. Traditional religion has often muddled the issue by preaching on the sin of gambling. There is nothing immoral about games of chance. If one has the means and wants to be entertained by picking horses or playing roulette, then let that person

enjoy himself or herself in clear conscience. However, it
may become a source of spiritual limitation if the gambler
is not spending available funds in entertainment but is
desperately trying to make his or her fortune. It is a self-
delusive trap, for in an orderly Universe, there is simply no
way in which one can get something for nothing. Under
divine law, you receive as you have given, no more and no
less. If you feel you have been "down on your luck," don't
succumb to the temptation to try to "make it big" in some
game of chance. Your fortune begins with you, not with
the roll of the dice or with the winning number or with
any kind of lucky break. There is only one way in which
you can "change your luck" and that is by altering your
thoughts. How inadvertently and yet surely we corrupt the
ideals of children when by precept and by example we
teach them that life is to be found and experienced "out
there" in the world. Thus when they arrive at the age of
responsibility, they are urged to go out into the world to
"make their fortune." They are progressively introduced
to the idea of getting the breaks, of expecting success to
come in one great stroke of good fortune. And they set a
veritable mine field of traps for themselves, so that the
career frustrations, the layoffs, or the investment failures
are all the results of "bad breaks." How blessed are the
children who early in life are taught that their fortune
begins with them! They will grow into spiritually mature
adults who are confident that they have the potential in
themselves to set into operation the fundamental process

which will cause all things in the world to work for their good. They will know that their fortune is not something to find but to unfold.

Sophisticated religious beliefs to the contrary notwithstanding, the average person's living philosophy centers at a point somewhere between the belief in kismet, the inevitability of fate and destiny, and the luck of the draw, with a subtle effort to change that luck in every conceivable way. A farmer may install a horseshoe over the barn door. One may carry a special charm or amulet in one's pocket. Religious people are among the most superstitious, though they justify the practices as being a part of their religious teaching. Call them what you will, all the little charms, medallions, and figurines that people wear or carry or hang on their doorposts or dashboards are done essentially for good luck. They constitute an attempt to alter what Voltaire calls "the concatenation of events." However, life is not a game of chance. Your fortune is not influenced by caprice. It is determined by the shape of your consciousness. In *Julius Caesar,* Shakespeare puts into the mouth of Cassius the meaningful statement: "The fault, dear Brutus, is not in our stars, but in ourselves, that we are underlings."

It is always sad to hear someone insist that some ironic twist of fate has ruined his or her life. One man was dismissed from his job. The result is he is bordering on a complete mental collapse. He says, "My life is over. It is the end of everything." He talks of the lucky break he had in getting this job many years earlier. He wonders how his dismissal now could reverse the "stroke of good fortune that established me in my career." The problem is really quite obvious: he has established his whole career on the flimsy platform of chance. Time and time again he has repeated the words, "How lucky I was to get this job." In a very real sense, through all the years he has been working under a "sword of Damocles." For if you live in the belief of good luck as the key of getting ahead, then the other side of the coin is that bad luck can frustrate your progress. You simply cannot have one without the other. The man had set the trap for himself, and thus his bad fortune, too, began with him.

Your prosperity and success, and your good fortune, certainly may be influenced by changing conditions, but even then depending upon how you deal with them. However, your good is always deeply rooted in what Jesus called "the kingdom of God within." And when he said, "It is your Father's good pleasure to give you the kingdom," he was saying that your fortune is an unborn possibility of limitless life, and yours is the privilege of giving birth to it. As Walt Whitman sings, "Henceforth I ask not good fortune. I myself am good fortune."

A great idea that may help you to unlearn some of the errors of human consciousness is this: *I am a most important person to God, for I am God's living enterprise.* God is not off somewhere in space where you must strain to reach Him to get Him to work a miracle for you "if you are lucky." God is on your side. God has a stake in you. God is not someone to reach for but a presence to accept. Instead of dwelling on how difficult things are for you, turn often to the center of your being and relax in the assurance that you are God's living enterprise and that your good fortune is secure because it is God's good pleasure to give it to you.

Is it possible that a person may actually be a "Jonah"? In the Bible story, Jonah was thrown overboard because the crew attributed all its misfortunes to Jonah's unlucky influence. Al Capp had a classic cartoon character, Joe Btfsplk, who always dressed in black and wore a crooked hat and had a black cloud over his head. Wherever he went misfortune occurred: machines broke down; feuds broke out; hens didn't lay; weapons misfired; and everything unfortunate that could happen, did happen. Are these situations realistic? Very much so! Not that once a Jonah always a Jonah. But one can fall into the "black-cloud syndrome" so that "trouble comes in troops."

Perhaps it is a psychological corollary of the scientific principle of "entropy," considered to be a fundamental factor of the Universe. Entropy causes organized forms to gradually disintegrate into lower and lower levels of organization. It is the basis of the theory that the Universe is like a great machine running down and wearing out. In a personally symbolic sense, we slip into an entropic consciousness through synchronizing our thoughts with the negative thinking of the world. Misfortune follows misfortune under this "black cloud." However, the influence can be reversed.

It is interesting that there is mounting evidence for the existence of an opposite scientific principle, "syntropy," through the influence of which forms tend to reach higher and higher levels of organization, order, and dynamic harmony. Albert Szent-Györgyi, Nobel prize-winning biologist, refers to it as an "innate drive in living matter to perfect itself." And today many are calling attention to a psychological drive toward synthesis, toward wholeness and self-perfection. Again, in a personally symbolic sense, we rise into a syntropic consciousness as we keep our minds stayed on God.

When you are in charge of your mind, in the consciousness of oneness with the creative flow, when you are working with life instead of against it, when you are positive and loving and secure in the conviction of Truth, then you are under the "white cloud" (Psalm 91 calls it "the shadow of the Almighty"). In this consciousness, syntropy does its work: parking spaces open up for you; stocks go up as you buy; dishonest people are fair in their dealings with you; jobs appear; promotions come. It would appear that you are living a "charmed life." Actually, it is nothing more nor less than consciousness outforming itself.

And when you maintain an optimistic view toward conditions in the world and are incurably "bullish" toward the economy in general, regardless of what the economic "gloom casters" may be saying, then you carry your white cloud of syntropy out into the world. You become a positive and highly contagious influence for a condition of general prosperity. In a very real sense, you make a difference!

Remember, your fortune, your personal success, and your prosperity are not in the hands of some "fickle finger of fate"—nor are they determined by sudden changes in the economy. The answer is in your conditioned ability to form and shape the ever-present substance of the Universe. You can change your luck.

Resolve that you will chase off the black cloud of entropy. Paul gives the key (Phillips translation): "Don't let the world around you force you into its mold, but let God remold your mind from within." Establish yourself under the white cloud of syntropy. You will walk and work in a consciousness in which all things will really work for good. Even a job dismissal will turn out to be the best thing that has ever happened to you, as you are serendipitously directed into a new career. Some will call it luck. Just be sure you call it consciousness. Your fortune begins with you!

Henry Thoreau seems to sum it up for us in this quotation from his classic work *Walden:*

If one advances confidently in the direction of his dreams, and endeavors to live the life which he has imagined, he will meet with a success unexpected in common hours. He will put some things behind, will pass an invisible boundary: new, universal, and more liberal laws will begin to establish themselves around and within him; or old laws will be expanded and interpreted in his favor in a more liberal sense, and he will live with license of a higher order of beings.

CHAPTER 3

The Law of Visualization

One of the most important aspects of the study of Truth is training the eyes to see properly. Since infancy we have been using our eyes in progressive degrees of perceptiveness. However, a person is never really mature until he or she understands the basic process of visualization. We have been conditioned to believe that life is lived from outside-in. We see things "out there," and we react with attitudes and feelings about them. Without question, what we see is as it is. Seeing is believing! This may give rise to defeatist comments, such as, "What are you going to do? It's just the way things are!"

Sight is an interesting phenomenon. Things seen fall on the retina of the eye upside down, as in a camera. Through the nerve endings that are sensitive to light, we get the picture distributed over several recording points. However, by the miracle of vision, we do not see all the points; they are all transformed into one solid view. Even more, what the mind sees is not this solid picture that is communicated to the brain, but what your awareness has conditioned you to see. In other words, seeing is *not* believing; *believing is seeing!* You see things, not as they are, but as *you* are. Your perception is shaped according to your previous experiences, according to your faith, according to where you are in consciousness. When something in your world is awry—inharmony in the office, a business venture that is not working out, or a bank balance that is insufficient to meet current obligations—normally the first concern is to set things right. However, when you understand the law of visualization, you will realize that the greatest need is not to set it right but to see it rightly. Right seeing is one of the most important keys to the effective demonstration of Truth. More important than changing things "out there" is changing the way you see them. In the words of the medieval mystic Brother Angelus, "That thou seest, man, become too thou must; God, if thou seest God, dust, if thou seest dust."

Thomas Troward puts the process of visualization succinctly when he says, "Having seen and felt the end, you have willed the means to the realization of the end." Having conceived and deeply felt some thing or experience, you have actually created the condition in mind that makes a particular result inevitable. It is fundamental law.

One of the most effective ways in which we use this law of visualization, and also by which we can understand it, is in worry. Worry is based on the belief that some undesirable condition already exists. Worriers vividly picture in mind the undesirable condition they are worrying about. Thus, according to Troward, because they see and feel the end, they will the means to the realization of the end. This is why Job said, "For the thing that I fear comes upon me" (Job 3:25). Of course! Because in the fear and anxiety, he was visualizing the end and creating the means in mind for its manifestation. This is the way mind unvaryingly works.

A man who had the full care of his invalid mother tells of his experience with the negative use of visualization. He says: "For eight years I had been filled with fear that I would lose my job and be unable to continue with her expensive treatments. It was a source of perpetual worry in my mind." Eight years of visualizing a condition, constantly willing the means to the realization of the end! Because it is inexorable law, it might be a miracle if it did not happen as he had so persistently visualized it . . . and happen it did. He lost the job. How very sad! How unjust! Fortunately, he didn't listen to his pitying friends. For as a student of Truth, he belatedly discovered what he had been doing. He began to reverse the process, seeing himself in a secure and well-paying job. In time came new opportunities and eventual success. He freely acknowledges today that the whole experience was a turning point in his life, for he learned a great lesson in the discovery of how one can creatively misuse a fundamental metaphysical law.

This is why Jesus said, "Do not judge by appearances, but judge with right judgment" (Jn. 7:24). Politicians are known to "view with alarm" as they evaluate the condition of the economy. Economic forecasters may also predict chaos in the marketplace. However, you have a choice. You can decide where you are going to throw the weight of your consciousness. And the welfare of the nation as a whole is determined by the attitude of "we the people." More and more economists are coming to agree that this word *economy* does not refer to a monolithic entity but rather to a financial climate chiefly influenced by the collective consciousness of the populace. This is why the economist has such a difficult time predicting economic trends, because no one really knows how two hundred million people are going to feel tomorrow morning. There is a growing awareness that the "jawboning" of a leader has a stronger impact on the economy than any form of government regulation, and that the whole economy could be swiftly turned around if the majority of the population would engage in positive thinking—seeing abundance everywhere—thus willing the means to the realization of the end.

Thus when Jesus said, "Do not judge by appearances, but judge with right judgment," he was saying that if we live in the belief that our experience is totally dependent on what happens to us, we become tentative, cautious, even a little paranoid, and every changing condition has the power to "pull our strings," to determine how we are going to think or feel or act. For instance, if our basic concerns are financial, then the daily Dow Jones report may well become our personal mood-meter, giving us faith or fear, joy or depression. It is a terrible way to live, yet it is probably true that it is the way most people do live.

However, if you really believe that life is lived from within-out, and if you persistently establish yourself in the consciousness of oneness with divine substance, then your perception of things will reflect an attitude that is "bullish" (optimistic). And, having seen and felt the end, you have willed the means to the realization of the end . . . for you. And it will work for you, no matter what happens in the world "out there." Psalm 91 (KJV) states the process emphatically: "He that dwelleth in the secret place of the most High [holding to the vision of oneness] shall abide under the shadow of the Almighty [the protective umbrella of consciousness]." More than this, "A thousand shall fall at thy side, and ten thousand at thy right hand; but it shall not come nigh thee."

What Jesus calls *right judgment* is "concentrical seeing," seeing from within. It is not settling on things as "just the way they are," but visualizing them as they can be. Of course you read the papers and are aware of conditions as they are. But it is important to keep a clear perspective of who *you* are. You are not simply an unthinking reactor to conditions. You are a creative person with your own unique relationship with the divine flow. You are always one with the source of boundless ideas, creativity, and success.

Now, let's be clear on what we mean by visualization. We do not suggest that you sit around imaging bags of gold. There is a widespread practice of what is called "treasure mapping," where one naively cuts out pictures from magazines that suggest the image of affluence and success and pastes them on a carefully designed poster to be displayed where it will regularly impress itself on one's subconscious mind, in a patently gross materialization of a beautiful spiritual law, one is subtly misled into the worship of mammon. It is like removing the lenses from your glasses and replacing them with gold coins. You may feel rich seeing only gold, but you will see precious little else.

This isn't what we are referring to. We are not talking about seeing things (cars, houses, jobs, jewels, and so forth), but rather seeing *from* a consciousness of ever-present substance, which will become the magnetic force that draws the things to you but without any of them ever becoming the object of your life. Jesus said, "Blessed are the pure in heart, for they shall see God" (Mt. 5:8). Not literally see God "out there," for "no man hath seen God at any time." (Jn 1:18 KJV). You see God as you see rosy hues when you look through rose-colored glasses. You see from God-consciousness. You project that consciousness.

So, when you are centered in oneness with God-substance, you see through substance-colored glasses. In a very real sense, to see abundance everywhere is to turn on the lights, which enables you to see allness even within illness and all-sufficiency even in lack.

L. P. Jacks, distinguished British philosopher, says, "Spirit is matter seen in a stronger light." Thus, if lack or financial limitation of any kind appears, the need is to turn on more light. Jesus advised us to let our light shine! Take a moment to get centered in the Allness of substance and then turn your centered consciousness on the experience. This is not to blind yourself to the facts, but rather to "contemplate" the facts . . . "from the highest point of view," as Emerson said.

It is interesting that the Hebrew word from which we get the word *eye* is *ayin*, which literally means "fountain." This suggests a powerful insight. Sight is not simply a matter of registering what we see out there, and "seeing is believing." It is that, but so much more. True seeing is a flow of consciousness, flowing like a fountain from within. Thus *where* you are in consciousness has everything to do with *what* you see in experience. If you have a sense of affluence, a sense of the omnipresence of substance, you are going to place that stamp on everything you see. It is not just that you will see things in a certain way, but your high-level, God-centered seeing has a formative power, having much to do with what actually happens in your world.

A little girl was looking out the front window of her

home, sobbing convulsively as she watched her brothers drag the lifeless body of her dog, which had just been struck down in the street, into the yard for burial. The Quaker father stood lovingly by, his arms comfortingly around her. In time he led her to another window looking out into the garden, where the little girl was soon squealing with delight as she noticed new blossoms on a small bush she had previously helped to plant. Patting her tenderly, the Quaker father said, "You see, dear, thee was looking out the wrong window."

We live in a house of consciousness, and a lot of things go on out there in the world. The most prominent window is the TV screen. As you listen to (actually witness) the news, you are presented with a skillfully produced picture of a world of crime and poverty and economic flux. In recent years "the news" has become the No. 1 entertainment form. Stations vie with one another to present the most sensation. Even weather reports are so over dramatized as to become almost worthless as forecasts. The problem is, when it comes to economic reports, because we are accustomed to being manipulated by what we see out this TV window, they become "self-fulfilling prophecy." What am I saying, that we shouldn't watch the news? Not at all. One may want, even need, to be informed. Just keep in mind that what you are seeing is the *appearance* of things. You have the right, perhaps even the responsibility, to put your own stamp of God-consciousness upon everything you see and hear. The important Truth is that if you are manipulated by the news, then you become a part of the world's problems; but if you look out the window of Truth and project a fountain of light and love, then you are a part of the solution. You become a peacemaker and a prosperity shaper.

In all the many ways in which you touch or are touched by life, it is important to be sure you look out the right window. Dorothea Brande says we should always act as if it were impossible to fail. To be ambitious for prosperity and yet to be manipulated by the economic indicators so as to repeat a common cliché like "we are in a terrible recession" or to desire healing and yet to talk about the "bug" that is going around may be compared to trying to reach east while traveling west. There is no philosophy in the world, certainly no metaphysical teaching, that can lead one to personal prosperity or success who is forever looking out the wrong window and indulging one's emotions in feelings of negativity and gloom.

The secret of achieving prosperity lies in so vividly keeping yourself centered in the inner focus of affluence that you literally exude the consciousness of it. This is often called the "prosperity consciousness." It is not something you gain through repeating prosperity affirmations over and over. It is getting yourself centered at the root of reality within. You see abundance, not dollar signs, not things, not pots of gold at the end of a rainbow. For the rainbow is seeing the storm through the raindrops. You see the appearance of whatever the need may be through the awareness of substance. You become a purveyor of the prosperity flow.

As we have said, you do not see things as *they* are but as *you* are. You will always tend to act like the person you conceive yourself to be. This is your self-image. As Emerson says, you surround yourself with the image of yourself. If your self-image is faulty, you project its limitation into every experience. Many inadequate job situations are the direct results of a self-image of inadequacy being impressed on the job experience. But you can change the way you see yourself. This is what the new insight in Truth is all about.

Self-image psychology provides some helpful techniques. However, the approach often tends toward the superficial. The focus may be chiefly on the image you see in the mirror, with the autosuggestion of the image you would like to see there. It is an ego-centered attempt to be like somebody else, based on covetousness. You want to have the physical appearance, the suave manner, and material achievements of some other person. In a group-sharing experience, it soon becomes obvious that this person is saying, "I want to change my self-image because I don't like myself." However, there is no way you can get a new image that can change your life if you begin with self-rejection. The missing link in the practice of self-image psychology is the realization that you do not change your self-image by rejecting what you are but by *discovering* what you are.

You *are* already created in the image-likeness of God, not *can be* if you speak a lot of positive affirmations of Truth. Your true image is not something to get; it is a reality to discover. There is that of you that is the likeness of God. It is your "I AM-age." This is what you really are, what you have always been. You can never be less. Oh, you may identify yourself as less, and thus project that awareness into your life experience. You may go along in all your affairs seeing less and manifesting less. As the poet says, many persons die with all their music in them. But you can never be less than your "I AM-age," for you were created with your very own divine potentiality and the power to fulfill it in a prosperous and successful life experience.

How futile it is to try to *get* a success-image! God succeeds every time a child is born. You were born to achieve, to release your inner power, to fulfill your uniqueness. It is the "little spark of celestial fire that you may desecrate but never quite lose." You may be like the prodigal son, living riotously at the circumference of human experience, working with dollar signs in your eyes, forgetting who you really are. As Meister Eckehart says, the prodigal is in the far country but the Father is at home. The Father is the reality of you that is always at the center of your being, no matter how off center you may become in consciousness. It is interesting that in the parable the prodigal son does not say, "I am a terrible person! Perhaps if I go back home I will get a new self-image." No, the parable says very simply that "he came to himself" (Lk. 15:17). Then he went home, not in quest of his "I AM-age," but out of his conscious realization of it.

An official of a large bank was interviewing a man applying for a substantial loan. Eventually the banker rose and extended his hand across the table and said, "You have the right spirit; we'll stand behind you." Thus it always is! The wealth of the Universe is behind you when you have the right spirit, when you *see* yourself in the right context, when you project the right image. Not by rejecting what you are, but by celebrating your true "I AM-age."

Within you right now is the possibility of success and achievement. You can bank on it. And yet if you are anxious about a business deal or worried about your job, you are seeing failure as a possibility. And *having seen and felt the end, you have willed the means to the realization of the end*. It is a shocking Truth that we should never forget.

A successful industrialist once said, "It is just as easy to see yourself successful as it is to see yourself a failure, and far more interesting." It will pay you to do some soul-searching. If you discover that you have a habit of saying, "Just my luck! Things never work out for me," just remember that you are making a decree. Is this really the way you want things to go for you? Why not make a positive declaration? It is just as easy, and so much more beneficial. Why not synchronize yourself with the divine flow and celebrate your "I AM-age" and affirm: *I see myself experiencing great success, for I am born to win*. It is not that by voicing these words you make something happen. But through the consciousness implied in the words, you begin to will the means to the realization of the end.

Experimental psychologists have proved that the human nervous system cannot tell the difference between an "actual" experience and the experience imagined in detail. Some years ago an interesting experiment was conducted at the University of Chicago. A number of students were divided into three test groups. First, they were tested for proficiency at throwing basketballs at a hoop. Then, the first group of students was told to go home and forget all about the test. The second group was told to come back to the gym one hour a day for thirty days and practice shooting baskets. The third group was told to find a quiet place at home where, one hour a day for thirty days, they were to imagine themselves throwing basketballs at the hoop.

At the end of thirty days the students were assembled again in the gym for a retesting. The first group, as expected, showed no improvement. The second group, after thirty hours of practice, showed an improvement of 24 percent. Obviously practice does improve one's skills. However, the interesting revelation came from the third group who had not touched a basketball but had imagined themselves shooting baskets. This group, we might call them the "imagineers," showed an increase in proficiency of 23 percent. Their improvement very nearly equaled those who had practiced every day.

It may seem beyond belief, but it is a fact that you can test for yourself. In sales work, you can prepare yourself for a good day by imagining yourself giving an effective sales "pitch" and actually see the customer signing the order. As a secretary, you can visualize error-free work being handed on time to an appreciative employer. As a golfer, an actor, or a violinist, you can spend leisure moments in "imagineering," with tremendously beneficial results. Whatever your lifework, wherever you have a need for improvement, try it. The law of visualization works.

Now, of course, this all requires mental discipline. *Positive thinking* is the popular term. However, we do not mean sitting around mouthing a lot of cheerful platitudes, such as, "Everything is going to be all right." The fact is, everything will not be all right until you achieve a consciousness of all-rightness. Much so-called positive thinking is little more than wishful thinking, voicing a lot of Pollyanna words that you really don't believe. You say them because that is what you think a Truth student should do. But positive thinking does not make creative power, nor does it change either God or conditions. It is a matter of synchronizing yourself in mind with the flow of the infinite. The ideal, of course, is to think the kinds of thoughts that lead to the kinds of conditions that you want to see manifest in your life.

A sales manager tells the story of a young salesman for whom he had high hopes. He put him in a territory that his company considered to be their best. At the end of the year he had earned about $25,000 in commissions. The people in the main office were upset because they felt this territory should produce enough business to earn at least $75,000 in commissions. So the sales manager was told, "Get rid of this man; he's ruining our business." But the manager didn't have the heart. Instead, he put him into their poorest territory, hoping the man would find himself, or else that he would quit in discouragement. By the end of the year the man had again earned about $25,000. This was considered so good for the territory that it was assumed that the young man had finally gotten it together. They put him back in the good territory, where again he earned $25,000. It is a classical example of the influence of a self-image. He sees himself as a $25,000-a-year man. Thus consciousness works like a governor on the speed of a car.

Now the young man is not lazy, for he had to work exceptionally hard to make a go of the poor area. He really wants to succeed. But he is seeing life out of a distorted self-image. Somehow he has not been able to say "yes" to greater success. If someone had tried to tell him that he had the ability to do much better, he might say, "I know I should, but . . ." There it is . . . *but*, a three-letter word signifying self-limitation. The fact is he is a divided person. Consciously, he wants to succeed, but his negative self-image simply will not allow it. Paul's soliloquy sums it up: "For what I would, that do I not; but what I hate, that do I" (Rom. 7:15 KJV).

The young man's excuse is ". . . but." It is like the person who says, in explanation for his poor performance on a job, "I was awake all night worrying." He says it as matter-of-factly as saying, "It rained all night." But it is *your* mind. And the *you* who has the mind has the power to control the thoughts and images that hold forth in the mind. It's an old cliché: Stand guard at the door of your mind. Don't allow negative thoughts to stand unchallenged. And "set a seal upon your lips." If you catch yourself in a negative proclamation, such as, "I can just imagine how bad things will be!" come right back with something like this, "Hey, that's a great affirmation. Let's repeat it three times for emphasis." It should help you to realize how ridiculous you are being. A speech teacher cuts in on students when they have hesitant "and er's" in their speeches. She says, "If you haven't anything to say, don't say it!" And for all of us who say negative things that we really do not want to see manifest in our lives, "If you haven't anything positive to say, then don't say it."

As you diligently work to think the positive thought, speak the constructive word, and hold the creative success-images in mind, your whole life will begin to vibrate with the dynamic power of prosperity. The law is, you can have all you can expect and accept. This was the eternal Truth given to Abraham: "Lift up now thine eyes, and look from the place where thou art northward, and southward, and eastward, and westward: For all the land which thou seest, to thee will I give it" (Gen. 13:14–15

KJV). And it is a relevant message for you today: whatever you can really visualize as being possible in your life, if you can believe (which we will discuss in the next chapter), you can achieve. Again, *having seen and felt the end, you have willed the means to the realization of the end.*

In Greek mythology, Pygmalion, King of Cyprus, carved a statue of marble, a figure of a woman so beautiful that every woman envied it and so perfect that the sculptor fell in love with it. He adorned it with flowers and jewels and spent day after day in love and adoration. Finally, the gods took pity on him and breathed into it the breath of life, and that which he had created became alive and real. It is a beautiful love story of ancient times with a profound lesson in living for today: dare to conceive of greater things for yourself. Dare to see yourself as strong, confident, capable, successful, and possessed of the patience and stability to keep on moving in the direction of your dreams.

> Dream lofty dreams, and as you dream you shall
>   become.
> Your vision is the promise of what you shall one
>   day be.
> Your idea is the prophecy of what you shall at last
>   unveil.
>   —*James Allen*

CHAPTER 4

If You Can Believe

"**A**ll things are possible to him that believeth" (Mk. 9:23 KJV). This is a tremendous promise with far-reaching implications. However, what does it mean to believe? Faith is not a constant. It means different things to different people. Certainly it is a fundamental mind power that is basic to the realization of prosperity. But we need to get a clear awareness of the faith process and how to set it to work for us.

When Jesus said "to him that believeth," it is normally presumed that he meant to one who believes in God. The religion of many persons consists simply in a profession of "I believe in God," though they rarely bother to ask themselves what they mean by God. Sydney Harris, the syndicated columnist said, "My father didn't believe in God, but God believed in my father." Many of his readers took offense. He meant that his father was not religious in a creedal sense, but he believed in life. He was a good person who walked by faith and acted out of love. God is not a superperson "out there" to whom we pray and from whom we beg favors. God is a life process by which we live. Emerson suggests that when you break with the God of tradition and cease from the God of the intellect that God will fire you with the Presence. There is no way that you can really begin to understand "spiritual economics" or to make it work in your life until you are free from the sense of God "up there" and on fire with the awareness of the Presence. God is not the Grand Man of the heavens, a great purser of accounts and disburser of divine substance. God is the transcendent whole of things of which you are an individualized part.

The whole Universe of innate substance is centered in you. There is nothing you can do to add to that or take away from it. And this centering, as far as God is concerned, is the same in all persons. That leads to the inescapable thought-shocking conclusion that the Universe was no more centered in Jesus than it is in you. Of course, that doesn't explain the quite obvious difference. Jesus in his disciplined consciousness was centered in the Source, while we are usually centered in various levels of limitation.

However, Jesus clearly said that you can do all that he did if you can believe, if you can center yourself in the creative flow, as he was always so centered. This suggests an excellent definition for the word *faith*, consciousness centered in the universal Source. Religious teachings and teachers have conditioned us to think of faith as a magic catalyst that makes God work for us. In no way does faith make God work nor does it release some kind of miracle power. Faith simply tunes into and turns on the divine flow that has always been present.

If you have a rheostat on your dining room light switch or if you recall the dimming of the lights in a theater, you have a good example of how the divine flow works. When you turn the rheostat up, you get more light; when you turn it down, the power flowing through the bulb is reduced, which results in less light. There is no miracle involved when the room is suddenly flooded with light. The power is present all the time, whether the rheostat is high or low. A turned-down rheostat is like a consciousness of lack that restricts the flow of substance. The turned-up rheostat is like a "faith-centering" that opens the way to an experience of affluence. Perhaps this is an oversimplification, but it may help you to understand the principle and the process involved.

Overzealous teachers and writers talk of the "magic of believing" and of the "miracle works of faith." It is understandable. They are excited about the role that faith plays in demonstrating prosperity. However, we must emphasize again: faith deals with law, not caprice. Thinking of magic and miracles may mislead you into dealing with some fortuitous turning of the wheel of fortune. God-substance is an ever-present, creative resource that must flow forth when you create the conditions which make the result inevitable.

Don't miss this vital insight. Faith is not a vague process of believing *in* something, much like a rote-learned confession of "I believe in God." It is, rather, a positive act of *turning on* something. The power is already within you, for you are the power being projected into visibility *as* you. You see, saying that you have faith in something, even faith in God "out there," suggests reaching and supplicating, touching a magic button that does not relate to your wholeness at all. The ideal is not "believing *in*" but "believing *from*." You begin with the assumption of the Presence in which you live and have being. Your faith is an activity that goes forth from this base. It is a believing attitude that is made real and creative by reason of your attunement with the creative flow.

The question may be asked, Do you really believe that faith can change things? There *is* a changing process, like light streaming into the room when you open the drapes. However, faith doesn't change the nature of reality any more than opening the drapes changes the nature of light. Faith tunes in to reality and releases the "imprisoned splendor."

In pre-Columbian times, the people believed in a flat world, but the world was still round. Their belief in a flat world did not change the round world one bit. Later, in the years following the discoveries of Columbus and Magellan, to believe in a round world did not require making changes in the flat world. Thus there is a sense in which faith doesn't really change things at all. It changes the way you relate to them. There is always an all-sufficiency even within the insufficiency. Your faith can relate to the whole or the partial. And it will be as you believe.

When you pray for prosperity, your faith does not magically create bags of gold at your feet. This is not the way of divine law. Actually, your faith has already been involved in your condition, as with the turned-down rheostat. You may have been believing in lack, and thus you have experienced lack. As you recenter your thought in the awareness of abundance, you turn up the rheostat, as it were, and become more synchronized with the process of eternal substance, which then flows forth in your experience in perfectly natural ways: increases in salary, higher investment returns, and other improvements.

Abundance is an ever-present reality. This fundamental Truth is the base on which all prosperity programs must build. Financial stringency of any kind is likened to the flat world. It is where you are in consciousness. But there is abundance for you right where you are, even as there is a round world within the flat world. The one simply transcends the other. This is what "transcendental" means. We are not talking about two different worlds, but about two ways in which you perceive and lay hold of the one world—the world in which you have lack and unemployment and hardship and the world of ever-present

limitless substance. If you have been believing in darkness, the drapes are tightly closed, and you have been experiencing darkness in your room. As you recenter your
awareness in positive faith, you open the window to the
light of Truth and it is as Isaiah suggests, "Behold, my ser-
vant shall prosper, he shall be . . . lifted up, and shall be
very high" (Is. 52:13).

The most widespread disease of our time may well be
"I-can't-itis." It is contracted by many of us early in life
from our elders. Society has made a song of it that has neither rhyme nor reason, but it may be heard everywhere:

> I can't because I am poor.
> I can't because I am sick.
> I can't because I do not have the ability.
> I can't because there is no opportunity.
> I can't because I am too old.
> I can't . . . I can't . . . I can't.

Few persons use more than a small part of the tremendous God-power within. You can alter the pattern of
harping on the same old "I can't" tune. Actually, there
can be no progress in the realization of prosperity until
you do so. It calls for knowing, really knowing, that
you are a spiritual being, living in a limitless spiritual
Universe, endowed with the whole potential energy
flow of the Universe. In most cases, the problem is
faulty self-evaluation. For instance, you may say, "I am an

average sort of person." This leads to the subconscious acceptance of the "wisdom of the world" which proclaims, "The chances of success for the average person in this enterprise are about one in seven." But why be an average person? All the great achievements of history have been made by strong individuals who refused to consult statistics or to listen to those who could prove convincingly that what they wanted to do, and in fact ultimately did do, was completely impossible. Let go of "I can't" and begin to identify yourself as God's living enterprise. You are not just an average person. You are *you*, a unique individualization of the universal creative process. Affirm for yourself: *I can, because I AM!*

Of course, you do live in the world of change and you may well have occasional pressing needs. The insight of Truth should not cause you to refuse to admit having them. The important thing is that a need has no built-in limitations. There are only limiting thoughts about it. If the Alps had looked as formidable to Napoleon as they did to his advisors, he would never have attempted crossing them in midwinter. But he displayed the focus of his consciousness when he said, "There shall be no Alps!" He wasn't denying their existence, only their impassibility. You may say of some overwhelming difficulty, "There is no way!" And there may be no way to human sense. Again, all things are possible to God and to you in God-consciousness. The Napoleons of science and industry and space technology have faced the "Alps" of insurmountable obstacles by implying "there shall be no Alps!" And so can you.

Right where you are in your present level of development, there is a limitless resource of wisdom and guidance, of ability and creativity, and of substance and supply through which you can do, and do superlatively well, all that needs to be done . . . if you can let go of limited self-identifications . . . if you can believe. The word *develop* is interesting in that it does not mean adding to or putting on something. It is related to the word *envelop*, which means to enclose. Thus "develop" means to unfold. Developing a prosperity consciousness is not achieved by "programming the mind" with an array of pat "statements of Truth." You *are* rich, not because you decree it over and over, but by reason of your spiritual inheritance. You are now as spiritual as you can ever be. You may increase your awareness of your true nature, which will in turn increase your flow of substance. You will not get prosperity out of a book, this one or any other. Prosperity comes from consciousness which unfolds from within. You will be amazed at the wonderful things that will begin to unfold for you as you develop a more positive image of yourself and as you recenter your faith in the all-accomplishing power of the divine process within you.

Occasionally a student of Truth will say: "I have worked so very long and hard to develop understanding. How long do I have to work at it until I arrive at the place where it just automatically works for me?" The thought is so understandable yet so naive. Ask the great athlete or the concert pianist or the successful actor if they have arrived at the place where they need no further practice. They will tell you that the higher you climb in proficiency and public acceptance, the greater the need for practice. You will note that even Jesus went regularly up into the mountains to pray to "practice the Presence of God."

There may be times when you say to yourself, "But this problem is *really* beyond solution. After all, I am only human; what do they expect?" But you are not *only* human. You *are* human, of course; but the human of you is a shell that encloses the divine of you. You can make your own personal breakthrough and release the tremendous possibility of your own divinity. This is the progressive unfoldment that you will experience as you diligently practice identifying yourself as a limitless expression of an unlimited Universe.

Do you find it conceivable that, when Jesus began to experiment with the creative power of faith, he may at times have been challenged even beyond his capacity to believe? Would it shock you to consider the possibility that something within him, the last vestiges of human consciousness, might have said "You can't heal this blind man . . . or provide a meal for this great throng of people. You wouldn't know how"? If you have been conditioned with the idea that Jesus was "very God," it may be hard for you to believe that early in life Jesus had the same basic difficulties of growing up as you had. Remember

Paul said that he was tempted in all ways, such as we are. In other words, he achieved mastery by personal development and practice, practice, practice. He said, in effect, "I have overcome the world, the flesh, and the devil." Doesn't that clearly suggest that he had something to conquer, some personal growth to achieve?

The great piano virtuoso Paderewski was once playing before an audience of the rich and the royal. After a brilliant performance, an elegant lady waxed ecstatic over the great artist. She said "Ah, Maestro, you are a genius!" Paderewski tartly replied, "Ah yes, madam, but before I was a genius I was a clod!" What he was saying was that his present acclaim was not handed to him on a silver platter. He, too, was once a little boy laboriously practicing his scales. And even at his peak, behind every brilliant performance there were countless hours of practice and preparation.

A needy person once knelt down before Jesus, saying, "Good Master." Jesus cut in abruptly, saying, "Why callest thou me good? none is good, save one, that is, God" (Lk. 18:18–19 KJV). He never seemed to lose sight of the fact that while people thought he was God-become-man, he knew he was man becoming God. We miss the whole meaning of Jesus' life unless we see it as a growth process and that before he achieved Christ mastery, he was Jesus, the pensive lad who wondered and dreamed on the hillsides of Galilee. He did not say, "I am more divine than you are. What I do comes by divine dispensation, but for you it will take a miracle." No, he said, in effect, "I have overcome the world by proving the power of faith and the inherent potential within man. If you believe in the creative flow of the Universe as I have done, then you can do all that I have done . . . and greater things shall you do."

The faith required to demonstrate prosperity is not simply a pious pronouncement. Faith is expectancy. You do not receive what you want; you do not receive what you pray for, not even what you say you have faith in. You will always receive what you actually expect. Sometimes, after people have experienced modest outworkings as a result of their prayer efforts, they may say, "Well, it is about what I expected!" They may only be trying to cover their wounded egos, but they are telling much about their faith. How many people go through life in this consciousness, holding a tin cup under the Niagara of God's plenty! It is a "small-fry expectancy" that usually manifests as a string-saving, make-do, can't-afford-it level of consciousness. It is marginal living at best. Some people even prepare for the worst so they will not be disappointed. And, of course, they rarely are. What a weak and insipid kind of life expectancy! It is what we might call "in tune with the indefinite."

It is important to know that the creative process is at work in you all the time, not just when you are "having faith." Infinite Mind is an activity that is constantly at work within you, not just when you are affirming healing or prosperity prayers. Sometimes people pray in tones that suggest trying to awaken God, urging God to get on the job. But it really works the other way: "Awake thou that sleepest" (Eph. 5:14 KJV). It is you who are asleep to your God-potential, which is always present. Unless you begin to understand God as principle, you will go on living marginally. The universal principle is "before they call I will answer" (Is. 65:24). In the great unity of all life, when you have a need, the answer is already moving on its way toward you. Before you formulate a desire in mind, it is God in you desiring. Before you have an urge to do something or embark upon a project, there is a moving of Spirit in you, prompting you in that direction.

When you understand the "cosmic origin of desire," the role of faith takes on a whole new meaning. It is not a matter of "Gee, I just wish I had enough faith to do this thing." If there is a need, there is an answer in Infinite Mind, and the need reveals that the answer is already on its way to you. Thus faith is not an attempt to demonstrate the magic of picking yourself up by the boot straps. Faith is your consent. It is saying "Yes!" to the outforming of the creative process. You may think this is making faith too simple. It *is* simple! There is nothing complicated about it. It deals with an inexorable force, like turning on a light. It is simple, but it is not easy. There is a discipline of consciousness required and the commitment to practice the Presence constantly. Yet the truth is, faith is saying "Yes!"

The exciting message of Truth is you can have all you desire. It is a concept that raises a lot of false expectations and gives rise to many objections. You may say "I certainly have desired many things that have not been realized." But we have not really listened to our desires, because our consciousness is too often centered in sense appetites and covetous urges. A true desire is not to *have* but to *be*. We are whole creatures in potential, and the true purpose of desire is to unfold that wholeness, to become what we can be. As Goethe says, "Desire is the presentiment of our inner abilities, and the forerunner of our ultimate accomplishments."

Unfortunately, some New Thought teachings of prosperity have been centered not in wholeness and spiritual well-being, but in the crassest kind of materiality. The "all things are possible" promise is met with the covetous gleam of dollar signs in the eyes. Techniques are offered by which to "treat"—work the principles—for the high-powered job, the luxurious country home, the expensive foreign car. "Just treat for it, and you will get it."

One woman recently said, "God wants me to wear sable; after all, I'm the child of a king." It is a common materialistic rationalization. The fact is, God does not want you to wear sable; God wants you to be stable. The impetuous, thing-oriented desire for sable may come from a sense of personal inadequacy, a lack of spiritual stability. The creative process seeks to express in you as a stable, well-balanced, prosperous person. But prosperity, you see, is spiritual well-being.

This is not to say that you cannot have fine things, for you can, and you should. When you have a balanced consciousness centered in the ever-present substance of God, the things will come easily as they are needed. It is a matter of priorities: "Seek first his kingdom" (Mt. 6:33). In other words, the first step should be not to treat for things but to get centered in the divine flow. God knows nothing of cars or jobs or fur coats or country homes. God is substance. And this substance will flow forth in your life in keeping with your consciousness of wholeness.

The danger in constantly working to demonstrate things, which the naive student of metaphysics is inclined to want to do, is that one tends to become an "economic hypochondriac." There is always something more to demonstrate. The magazines and catalogs are full of alluring pictures that whet one's covetous feelings. How easily one's life can become dominated by things—the work to get them, the effort to care for them, the need to buy insurance to protect them. On and on it goes. And there is always something more to yearn for. After all, this is what prosperity is supposed to mean. Or is it?

Students love to talk about all the demonstrations of prosperity they have made. Yet there is a sadness about it, for there is an implied emptiness and the frantic attempt to fill it. So the person makes innumerable demonstrations of prosperity and yet never finds prosperity, never experiences wholeness in Spirit. The mystic ideal, so often missed, is really very simple: build on the awareness of ever-present substance and expand your faith in the stability of your own inner wholeness. The things will come too, and in abundance. But they will come out of the *expanse* of your wholeness, not at its *expense*.

Faith is really your consent to let your own uniqueness unfold and to let that which is attracted by your uniqueness manifest in your life. Thus when Jesus said, "All things are possible to them that believe," he did not say that a swan can become a duck or that a nonmusical person can become a concert pianist. You cannot become something that is not the outforming of your own inner potential. You can only *be* you. However you can unfold more of the you that may have been long frustrated.

Many people are covetously influenced to seek to "become like her" or to "have what he has." But if, through mind dynamics, you achieve that which is not the outforming of your uniqueness, you may lose even if you win. As with the problem in transplant surgery where "rejection syndrome" prevents the tissue from taking hold, so you are unable to hold or to fully experience that which has not come out of your own pattern. The important thing is to know yourself, have faith in the cosmic process that will unfold in you like the life force unfolds in the lily of the field which toils not nor spins, and yet "Solomon in all his glory was not arrayed like one of these" (Mt. 6:29).

Now, having said all this, let us re-emphasize the Truth that you can grow, you can improve, you can be prosperous, you can succeed, if you can believe. When you say "Yes!" to the creative flow within you, you begin to experience I-am-positive-I-can attitudes, which turn on the power and skills needed to accomplish. When you believe you can do it, the how-to-do-it develops. This is the way the creative process in the individual works. On the other hand, disbelief is a negative power that frustrates or turns off your inner potential. If you doubt something enough, the mind will attract all kinds of reasons to support the disbelief.

In his classic work *Wind, Sand, and Stars*, St. Exupery tells the story of a pilot who was downed in the rugged, snow-blocked region of the Andes. He trudged through the snow for days, only to find his way hopelessly blocked by a yawning crevice in the ice. He quickly concluded that he had three choices: (1) give up and die of exposure, (2) make an attempt to jump across the fissure, knowing full well that it was impossible to do so, or (3) convince himself that he could jump across and make an attempt out of that conviction. When considered in this kind of logic, the choice was clear. So he backed away a few yards, closed his eyes in a moment of inner communion, then, loudly shouting, "I can! I can!" he ran and jumped and barely reached safety on the other side. Trudging off down the mountain, he was finally found and saved.

Now faith was no magic bridge. This was no miracle of God picking him up and depositing him bodily on the other side. What the man did was accomplished with his own concentrated mind and by special effort by his own muscles. But his believing attitude released a flow of energy from his own inner God potential. There are many stories of seemingly superhuman feats accomplished under emotional stress. We are all too ready to call them miracles. How much more in keeping with the ideal of the divinity of man to know that it is simply a matter of *opening out a way whence the imprisoned splendor may escape.* And as Jesus promised, "Greater works than these will he [you] do" (Jn. 14:12) *if you can believe.*

You may survey your situation today as concerns your financial needs or your job situation, obsessed with the problems of inflation, restrictive interest rates, or the threat of crippling depression. You may be totally discouraged, or you may carry on halfheartedly in the thought, What are you going to do? It's just the way things are. But there is much that you can do. You need not live marginally. You can achieve prosperity, if you can believe in the allness of God-substance ever-present and all-sufficient, abundantly able to meet any and every need in your life. Your potential to harness the flow of the Universe is the very law of your being. Even as the flick of a switch turns on the light by reason of the law of electricity, so your faith releases your success power by reason of the law of Spirit within you.

No miracles are required. It is the way you have been created. You are a rich and creative spiritual being. You can never be less than this. You may frustrate your potential. You may identify with that which is less than what you *can* be. But within you now and always is the unborn possibility of a limitless experience of inner stability and outer treasure, and yours is the privilege of giving birth to it. And you will, if you can believe.

CHAPTER **5**

The Grateful Heart

What is your most important asset? Conditioned as it is to materialistic values, your mind might begin weighing the relative usefulness of things. However, if you carefully search within yourself, you may come to the awareness that your most important asset is the conscious control of your own life. Nothing else can satisfy or fulfill unless you enjoy the freedom that comes from control of your inner world of mind and emotions.

> Oh, while I live, to be the ruler of life, not a slave, to meet life as a powerful conqueror, and nothing exterior to me shall ever take command of me.
>
> —*Walt Whitman*

Yet we do allow events, people, things, and economic conditions to take control of us.

Note, for instance, how many people have become slaves to the wild fluctuations of the economy. Ask them how they feel and they might very well say, "I will be able to tell you after I read the stock market returns," or ". . . after I see what my accountant comes up with." How we are manipulated by worldly conditions and values!

A man was told by his doctor that he had but six months to live. A shocking discovery of an incurable condition! One might expect him to have an emotional collapse. But not this man. He reported to work the next morning as usual. His co-workers heard about the pronouncement and were shocked. They hovered around, morbidly commiserating with him. Someone asked, "What will you do?" His reply, "I will do what I have always done: live with a grateful heart, one day at a time." And he could be grateful for the "is-ness" of life.

Actually, this crisis was more than ten years ago, and the man in question is very much alive and well, still living one day at a time with a truly grateful heart. It is not necessarily that the diagnosis was in error. Perhaps it is more a testimony to the healing influence of a controlled life sustained by an attitude of gratitude. The important thing is that these ten years have been creative years, not just a dreary existence in anticipation of doom. One might say, "Well, now at least he has something to be really grateful for. What did he have ten years ago?" But that is to miss the whole meaning of his demonstration. What his controlled life has proved is that thanksgiving is not just a reactionary emotion; it is a causative energy. It is an effective key by which anyone may "meet life as a powerful conqueror."

Let us consider this key as an important, though normally overlooked, element in the process of achieving prosperity. But first, a point of clarification: we usually consider gratitude and thanksgiving on the basis of obligation. For instance, someone does something for us and we feel obligated to show some kind of appreciation. Traditional religionists would insist that we owe it to God to give thanks for all our blessings. All this is good. We should be grateful. It is an important social grace. But even more, it is a requisite for high-level wellness.

Now, you know how people react if you are not grateful, but what about God? Will God be disturbed if you do not return thanks? Will God say of you, "Such an ingrate!" The fact is, it doesn't make any difference to God whether you give thanks or not. But it makes a lot of difference to you. God is too universal, too almighty, to be dependent on your thanksgiving. Meister Eckehart probably shocked his colleagues in medieval times when he said, "I never give thanks to God for loving me, because He can't help himself; whether He would or not, it is his nature to." You see, gratitude is not for God. You are not obligated to thank God for your life, for your job, for your prosperity. However, giving thanks is an important state of your consciousness that keeps you in an awareness of oneness with divine flow. When you understand this, you see that a grateful heart does not need something to be grateful for. One can be grateful with the same spontaneity as being happy. It simply flows forth from within and becomes a causative energy.

Paul gave some advice that has been puzzling to many persons. He said, in effect, "In all things give thanks." All things! Is this practical? Or even possible? Can you be grateful for inflation that constantly steals the value of your money? Can you give thanks for spiraling costs, for exorbitant interest rates, for personal financial crises? And how can you give thanks for lack and for unemployment? You don't! According to the law of consciousness, these things manifest in your life because in some subtle subconscious way you are frustrating the divine flow.

Let's look again at that puzzling statement of Paul's. Note that he does not say, "*For* all things give thanks." In the old-time religion, if you had pants with patches, you should thank God for the pants, patches and all. Poverty was a grace. We were told, "Be grateful for your little today, for you will have abundance by and by." In other words, you will have a great reward in heaven for being patient in your poverty today. It is a doctrine that has had a tragic, repressive influence on millions of people through the ages of Christian history.

What Paul does say is "*in* all things give thanks." In other words, despite the problems of lack, or even because of them, the need is to get yourself recentered in the awareness of the ever-presence of substance. And the most effective way to accomplish this is by thanksgiving. Paul is stressing the importance of the grateful heart, not simply an expression of gratitude for things, but a heart that is grateful (full of greatness). The man who had six months to live may have had little to be grateful for. But he was grateful because he had a great reserve of faith to give thanks *from*. This insight of the grateful heart is a dynamic key to personal prosperity.

It is a cosmic ideal that has been caught and taught by mystic teachers of all ages. Perhaps no one has articulated it better than Plato, who said more than 2500 years ago, "A grateful mind is a great mind which eventually attracts to itself great things." A tremendous insight! The grateful person is great because he or she has turned on all the lights within. You may say of someone, "He has so much, and he is so grateful." But by "Plato's law," it may be that he has so much *because* he is so grateful. The grateful heart actually opens the way to the flow and becomes an attractive force to draw to itself great things.

An English couple was visiting New York City for the first time. They came with some apprehensiveness because they had been conditioned with a vision of a sordid and crime-ridden city. Their host thoughtfully took them first to the observation deck of one of the city's highest buildings so they could get a lofty overview. It was a beautiful clear day, and they could "see forever." The visitors were delighted and surprised, giving them a very positive initial reaction. Later, in a tour of the city, the man remarked that he could not forget that view from the top. They had a wonderful weeklong stay and left singing the praises of the "loveliest, friendliest, and finest place we have ever been." All because of the initial high-level perspective.

It is a powerful insight to live by: Always get the view from the top. Before you react in negativity to people, conditions, or things, take a moment to lift up your eyes unto the hills. Contemplate all the changing, challenging experiences from the highest possible point of view. Regardless of the appearances of conflicts or limitations, see all things from the awareness of the allness of life and the ever-presence of substance. From the view from the top, you will see things creatively, leading to an attitude that is constructive and optimistic.

There is an old saying that a donkey may carry a heavy load of precious sandalwood on its back and never know its preciousness—only its weight. You may go through life feeling only the weight of circumstances, never able to appreciate the precious nature of life. Contrasting the view from the high building, it is like viewing the city from the sewer. With your head bowed down and your eyes fixed on the ground, you perceive a world of lack and limitation, and you attract to yourself conditions of financial chaos. How great is the need for the grateful heart that will attract to itself great things.

Some people, realizing the importance of the grateful heart, begin looking for things for which to give thanks.

However, they mistakenly start with the perspective of inadequacy and insufficiency, and thus they simply become more conscious of limitations. The result is, instead of counting their blessings, they count their envies: "He is so talented"; "She has so many lovely things"; or "I wish I had a lovely home like they have." As a result of this very subtle process, they develop, paradoxically, "ungrateful hearts."

To pray for prosperity out of a sense of complaint or discouragement is to effectively compound the problem. You may pray for improved financial conditions, but if you are feeling poor, your feeling is the consciousness you will be projecting. The grateful heart draws to itself great things. The ungrateful heart, the discouraged, complaining, covetous level of thought, will draw to itself limited things.

Theodore Roosevelt used to say, "Do what you can with what you have right where you are." So begin, not with subtle resistance for what you do not have, but with what you have—a job, no matter how inadequate; some money, even if you are down to the proverbial last penny. Get the view from the top. Remember that in Truth, there is abundance everywhere, so give thanks. This is not to say you should give thanks for a job that is unpleasant or for the last penny if your supply is totally inadequate. That would be to kid yourself and to be intellectually dishonest. Many people become confused at this point in the misunderstanding of Paul's statement: "Giving thanks always for all things" (Eph. 5:20 KJV). The job is not a symbol of misfortune, and the penny is not a symbol of lack. Both are evidence of the activity of Spirit manifesting in part. So you give thanks, not *for* these things, but *from* the awareness that there is always an all-sufficiency even within the insufficiency.

The classical example of this principle is the gospel account of Jesus dealing with five thousand hungry people. The disciples reported that the only provision they could find at hand was one boy's lunch consisting of five loaves and two fishes obviously inadequate to meet the need. Jesus, starting with what they had, took the boy's lunch in his hands and "looked up to heaven" (Lk. 9:16) and gave thanks. This was not reaching up to God, for he had once clearly said that the kingdom of heaven is within you. He was turning away from the appearance of lack and getting the view from the top. Again, he was not giving thanks *for* the inadequate lunch. No, he was giving thanks *from* that elevated consciousness, or the presence of abundance as was visually suggested by the loaves and fishes. There wasn't enough bread, but there *was* enough substance, for the whole of God-substance is present in its entirety at every point in space. How quickly we forget!

Next, Jesus did a strange thing: He *blessed* the available food. This power of blessing is not reserved for holy places or for specially ordained persons. It is an act of tremendous power that can be used by anyone. To find how extremely appropriate it was for Jesus to bless the boy's lunch, consult the dictionary. You will find that the word means "to confer prosperity upon." You are always projecting some kind of thought toward everything you have or hold. Sometimes it is negative, limiting, restrictive. But you can bless your home, your job, or your money supply, and thus confer a consciousness of abundance upon them. It is not something you *do* to these things. Rather it is a correction of the mentality that you are projecting to them. And the law is that things become to you that which you see them as being. So Jesus blessed the food, and it was distributed to the people in such abundance that there were twelve full baskets left over. A truly amazing, if not incredible, demonstration.

You may have always secretly wondered how this feat was accomplished. It is usually explained away as a "miracle of God." However, we have already established the view that God doesn't deal in miracles but with the orderly outworking of divine law. This is not to question the validity of the story, only to insist that whatever the process, it must be repeatable. We are perfectly willing to accept as universal law the process of limitless increase of substance out of a divine flow and under the influence of God-consciousness. However, some people may need to believe that God works through human hands.

A Bible scholar, Dr. George Lamsa, offers an interesting conjecture. He suggests the possibility that some merchants from surrounding towns, unable to join the throng for this transcendent experience with the Master, decided to pool their resources and send a few camel loads of provisions for the midday repast, as their gift to Jesus' great work. And this unsolicited gift of food arrived at the precise moment that Jesus was blessing the boy's lunch. It is, of course, highly credible. Certainly, when you pray for abundance in some time of need, you do not expect to have bags of gold deposited at your front door. You would anticipate the answer coming through a salary increase or some additional return on investments, and so on. Dr. Lamsa has fielded scores of questions attacking the blasphemy of his rationalization by coming back with a simple question of his own: "The Gospel account clearly says there were twelve baskets full of food left over. Where did those twelve baskets come from?" Of course, there is no answer.

Let us not get too involved in the mechanics of the process. The important thing is the evidence we do have: "He looked up to heaven" and gave thanks. In that moment of gratefulness, he became great and eventually attracted to himself great things. The grateful heart will always attract to itself in one way or another, through human hands or through wonder-working ways, the great things needed to solve the particular situation. It is an outworking that you can stake your life on.

A missionary to Africa has related the story of his work with a tribe that was mysteriously poverty-stricken, even though other tribes in the same region were relatively prosperous. He was curious about this strange phenomenon. He spent years researching all aspects of their culture. He came up with but one possibility: in their tribal language, they had no word with which to express gratitude. Perhaps, through some quirk of evolution, they had forgotten how to say thank you. He drew no conclusions, but he did ask a question: "Could this loss of the spirit of thanksgiving have been responsible for their poverty?" It is an interesting and revealing possibility. We might ask the same question of ourselves: "Could it be that our own financial problems may be the result of the loss, even temporarily, of a grateful heart?"

Some people might protest: "But you don't understand my situation. How can I be grateful in my financial dilemma?" This is precisely the time to "stir up the gift" of gratitude! Remember, it is not a reactionary emotion but a causative energy. You do not need something to be grateful for. You need only the desire to feel grateful. Invoke Plato's law: When you feel grateful, you become great, and eventually attract great things. The missionary all but concludes that we grow rich by thanksgiving, and we grow impoverished by losing the spirit of gratitude.

George Bernard Shaw once said, "God has given us a world that nothing but our own folly keeps from being a paradise." In other words, we live in a world that always has the potential for affluence. All the substance of the Universe, all the wealth that has ever manifested itself or ever will manifest itself in this world, is present right now. This is why Jesus said, "I came that they may have life, and have it abundantly" (Jn. 10:10). He means a life that is rich and fulfilled—healthy, prosperous, loving. Only our lack of perception, lack of the grateful heart, keeps us from experiencing it. We have the choice to be great or small. When we are grateful, we are great. When we become lax in the expression of gratitude, we become little people with little minds, leading little, inconsequential lives.

The man with six months to live was able to live gratefully because he had learned to live basically. You may talk about, plan for, and fret over the years ahead, but basically you have only one day, and as Carlisle says, you can make of this one day a dance, a dirge, or a life-march as you will. It is your day. You are alive in it. You don't need to wonder what the day will bring. It is an unfolding opportunity to express and to grow. You are in the express business, and growth is what it is all about. Of all people in all ages, no one has more reason for thanksgiving than you.

Take a moment right now to engage in the experience of gratitude. Close the book and your eyes and just *feel* grateful. Don't turn outward, casting about for things to give thanks for. Remember, it is not an emotional reaction to the blessings you can count; it is an energy you stir up within you that is causal. Resist the temptation to indulge such thoughts as, I would be grateful if I received that promotion and raise in salary. No qualifications, no ifs or whens. Just *feel* grateful. Let the spirit of thanksgiving flood your whole being with its healing warmth.

According to Plato's law, as you feel grateful, you become attractive, not only in your beauty and radiance, but in your relationships with people. More important, you release a vital energy that draws to you opportunities, employment, and a secure flow of substance. Everything begins to work in your life in an orderly and creative way. You may be so uplifted in the joy of thanksgiving that your consciousness easily gives vent to the activity of blessing. In your gratefulness of heart, you can *confer prosperity upon* all the many things, experiences, and people, whose performances have such a profound influence on your life. Bless the car you drive or the bus or train you ride. Bless the weather and the traffic. Bless your place of business or employment. Bless your employer and your co-workers. Bless your investments and your cash flow. Bless your home and family. Bless your friends and neighbors. Now, blessing exerts no magic power over these people, conditions, or things. In fact, it doesn't change them at all; it changes you, your thoughts and feelings, and the consciousness you project into your world.

Charles Fillmore says:

God is the source of a mighty stream of substance, and you are a tributary of that stream, a channel of expression. Blessing the substance increases its flow. If your money supply is low or your purse seems empty, take it in your hands and bless it. See it filled with living substance ready to become manifest. As you prepare your meals, bless the food with the thought of spiritual substance. When you dress, bless your garments and realize that you are being constantly clothed with God's substance. . . . The more conscious you become of the presence of the living substance the more it will manifest itself for you and the richer will be the common good of all. . . . Identify yourself with substance . . . and you will soon begin to rejoice in the ever-present bounty of God.

Keep alive the commitment to the view from the top. Keep centered in the feeling of thanksgiving. It is not just to be grateful for loving friends, for an affluence of wonderful things, and for divine order in everything that happens in your life. It is so much more. You are grateful from the root of reality that is evidenced by these things. Your thanksgiving is more than a response to what is happening around you or to you. It is a celebration of Truth, which becomes a causal assurance of a continuity of blessings, leading toward prosperity for you.

CHAPTER 6

Work and the Success Syndrome

When Jesus says, "And ye shall know the truth, and the truth shall make you free" (Jn. 8:32 KJV), he implies that our bondage in life is caused by our acceptance of erroneous beliefs. A Greek philosopher, Zeno, says, "The most important part of learning is to unlearn our errors." In the study of spiritual economics, nothing is more basic or more rife with mistaken beliefs than our attitudes toward work.

Why do you work? You may smile at the question, for it seems perfectly obvious that everyone works to make a living. However, if this is the only reason you can come up with, then it is one of the errors that needs to be unlearned. It is an attitude that may well be frustrating your creative flow.

What are you getting out of your work?

If you respond in terms of salary figures, fringe benefits, and executive "perks," then you are underpaid. Not that your employer is inadequately compensating you. That is something else. What we are referring to is that by the evidence of your narrowness of vision, you are shortchanging yourself.

Your prosperity will always be a reflection of your consciousness, the degree to which your thoughts are centered in the divine flow. You spend most of your life engaged in some kind of gainful employment; thus if your attitudes about work in general and your job in particular are not right, then truly you are working against yourself. You may seek diligently to demonstrate prosperity, but unless you unlearn your error thoughts about work, you will forever be out of "sync" with the creative flow of the Universe.

A German educator, Friedrich Fröbel, had a refreshingly positive sense of the cosmic process at work within the individual. How good it would be if his ideal of work could be stressed in our modern-day educational system:

> The delusive idea that men merely toil and work for the sake of preserving their bodies and procuring for themselves bread, houses, and clothes—is degrading, and not to be encouraged. The true origin of man's activity and creativeness lies in his increasing impulse to embody outside of himself the divine and spiritual element within him.

It is a tremendous realization. What if our young people could be graduated into their work life with a preconditioning of this awareness?

Work is, and should be so considered by every worker, a giving process. Jesus said, "Let not thy left hand know what thy right hand doeth" (Mt. 6:3 KJV). In other words, don't get trapped in the error of equating what you earn with the work you do. How easy and yet how mistaken it is to be influenced by the "another day, another dollar" syndrome. Let your work, whatever it may involve, be an outworking of the creative flow, engaged in through the sheer joy of fulfilling your divine nature. You will prosper, and you should do so, but it will not be because you have "made money" in your job. The work in the job is the means by which you build a consciousness of giving, which in turn gives rise to an outworking or "receiving flow." It is a subtle distinction but an extremely important one. If the left hand (receiving your pay) knows what the right hand does (the work of your job) then there is no real giving, only a bartering. This is "selling your soul for a mess of pottage." All the elements needed to fulfill the prosperity law for you are missing.

A distinguished professor at Harvard University once said, "The University pays me for doing what I would gladly do for nothing, if I could afford it." Most persons might laugh at his naïveté. However, what he is saying is that his work is not just a place to tediously make a living but an opportunity to joyously live his making. In other words, he is looking at his teaching work in terms of the privilege it gives him to grow as a person. And growth is what life is all about . . . not just paychecks and fringe benefits, but growth. It is probably true that the best living is "made" by those workers whose chief motivation is to give themselves away.

It is sad but true that the professor is unusual, for one of the greatest problems in the Western world today is "the great depression of worker attitudes." There has been a steady erosion of the old-fashioned work ethic, leading to a loss of the sense of work being done in the context of the whole person. Thus we can see everywhere great masses of people going off each day to a work that is drudgery, an empty and meaningless process of putting in time. Little is given beside what is required, and little is received besides a contracted-for salary. There may be three reasons for this depression of work attitudes:

1. The growing trend toward specialization through computerization and automated production, where few people do a whole job they can feel good about. Rapidly dwindling are the opportunities to work in places where you can commence with the basic materials and create something in which you can stand back and say, "Look what I did!"

2. The changing values of society where the "good job" has come to mean the high salary. This has led to "job-hopping" for work that will pay more money. People will often leave jobs they like to take a better paying job they really don't like at all.

3. The materialistic and gadget-conscious culture which deems as necessities more and more expensive things, which requires more and more money and the job as the place to earn it. This has led to what is called "moonlighting," where the worker may hold down two or more jobs in which he or she works all hours in order to try to keep up with a standard of living.

Work that is dealt with outside the whole person is a painful process engaged in "by the sweat of the brow." There is a tendency to deal with our work life almost as if it were a life sentence from which we may ultimately retire as time off for good behavior. Truly this confusion of work attitudes gives rise to all kinds of breakdowns: employment, financial, and even physical.

Personnel people often refer to individuals as entering the "labor market," as if they sell themselves and their services in exchange for the wherewithal to exist. And some people may describe a job that they have taken just to get by, by saying, "It's a living." In this consciousness, it is anything but a living. It might be more accurate to characterize it as a drab existence. And in the process of that kind of existence, those people may not only have subtle feelings of frustration and resentment, but as effectively as if they had put a rubber band around a finger, they are cutting off the creative flow. There is simply no way in which people can change their lives from indigence to affluence, until they alter some of their underlying thoughts and feelings toward work.

A sad spectacle that is seen all too frequently is when workers work for a paycheck for which they have done as little as they can get by with. They are creating all kinds of hidden frustrations for which they will have to pay the price because there is a spiritual law involved. They may think they can get away with slipshod work, fudging on their time sheet, and calling in sick to get a day off. And they may well get away *with* it; but they can never get away *from* it. The motivations that directed them to do these things is from a level of their consciousness. Ultimately, they will have to "pay the piper," for it is inexorable law.

Life is a growth process, and we grow through giving. Thus no matter what the circumstance, if we do less than our very best in what we may be doing, no matter what the recognition or reward, we are storing up what the Easterners might call "bad karma." We may wonder: "What is wrong in my life? Why can I not demonstrate prosperity?" Consciousness! "Whosoever hath, to him shall be given . . . whosoever hath not, from him shall be taken away even that he hath" (Mt. 13:12 KJV). It is fundamental law. There is no way that prosperity can be demonstrated outside the law of consciousness.

You may protest, "But I do all that I am paid for!" However, work should be an experience of growth. If you are not growing in the process of doing your work, then something must be wrong. Kahlil Gibran lays it right on the line: "If you cannot work with love but only with distaste, then you should quit your job and go sit at the Temple and beg alms from those who work with joy." A hard lesson, but an important insight into consciousness.

An effective commercial for one of the airlines says, "We have to earn our wings every day." Yes, and you have to earn the level of consciousness by which you are sustained and prospered . . . every day. You may say, "I have been on this job for years, and I know the work so well that I could do it with my eyes closed." And you probably can. But what is happening to you as a person? You must earn your wings, not to please your employer, but for your spiritual well-being. What you do in your work every day may not affect your salary, but it vitally affects your focus on consciousness that regulates the flow of affluence into your life. You might seriously consider making it a commitment. Every day as you commence your work, affirm for yourself: *I am going to earn my wings today!*

There is a common tendency to do a job skillfully and

just settle into a rut, typing the job and limiting yourself. One man was protesting to his employer that a person of far less experience had been promoted over him. He said, "Why, I have had twenty-five years experience on this job!" The wise employer replied: "That's not quite correct. You have had one year's experience twenty-five times over." He was doing the work, but he wasn't earning his wings; he wasn't growing. A corporation prospers by consciousness too, the collective consciousness of its workforce. We forget this when we deal with work schedules, computers, and automated processes. Thus if you, as just one worker, are lacking in the "alive, alert, awake, joyous, and enthusiastic" consciousness by which you do your job, certainly you are frustrating yourself, and you are not growing as a person. But what you should never forget is that you are not giving in that special way which adds to the growth of the company. Thus he who has is given more, even if it means promoting another worker over you. Consciousness works inexorably.

You may say, "But my job is not imaginative; there is no future in it." There is no job with a future in it; the future is in the one who does the job. When you do your work imaginatively, the job will become more meaningful and interesting, and you will become more effective in it. You can change your job, any job, if you change your attitudes about it. You may want to look elsewhere, to find a better job, but that can be an escape. It is the eternal hope of finding the pot of gold at the end of a rainbow. Of course, there could be a better job for you somewhere else, but the starting place in making the change is right where you are. "Agree with thine adversary" (Mt. 5:25 KJV) means settle with your adverse feelings. When you discipline yourself to earn your wings every day, one of two things will happen: (1) your consciousness will bring about a change in the job, making it right for you and you for the company, or (2) another job will open up for you where a transfer will be effected in a way that is beneficial to all concerned.

Refreshing is the holism of Ralph Waldo Emerson:

> No matter what your work, let it be your own. No matter what your occupation, let what you are doing be organic. Let it be in your bones. In this way you will open the door by which the affluence of heaven and earth shall stream into you.

It is a beautiful insight dealing with prosperity as a divine flow from within. When you work in the right consciousness, when your work becomes organically a part of your whole self, and when you do your work out of that commitment, no matter what other people do, no matter what the compensation may be, doing it for the health of your own soul, then you open the door by which the affluence of the Universe flows forth into your life. It is a beautiful realization, but how quickly you forget, going to the office, reading the morning paper over your cup of coffee, and then plunging into a meaningless job, which offers little more than various levels of boredom through the day. And if this is the attitude, then it follows as night follows day that there will be a problem of financial stringency in your life. It will do little good to run frantically to a Truth teacher asking for prosperity prayers. God can do no more for you than God can do through you. As the Quakers say, "When you pray, move your feet." In this case, move your hands. Begin to do what you do in the awareness that you are working with God for the releasing of your own "inner splendor." And when you earn your wings in consciousness, "the affluence of heaven and earth will stream into you."

In his classic work *The Prophet*, Kahlil Gibran says:

> When you work you fulfil a part of earth's furthest dream, assigned to you when that dream was born,
> And in keeping yourself with labour you are in truth loving life,
> And to love life through labour is to be intimate with life's inmost secret.

Life's *inmost secret* is the divine pattern in you which you can only really know when you are giving yourself in service. You can work for money and prestige and climb to the pinnacle of success and still not know yourself, thus seeking other avenues of escape such as alcohol and various kinds of addiction. All this is because your work does not satisfy you. And the reason it doesn't satisfy you is that you are not satisfied with or fulfilled in yourself.

However, when you are intimate with life's secret, your work becomes your calling. The word *vocation* comes from the Latin, meaning, "I call." Begin to think of your work as a calling. The creative process is calling, singing its song in you and as you. However, it is not your song but the will of Him who sent you. So the work becomes easy and fulfilling, and you become prosperous and successful in it. There is no pressure, for "the affluence of heaven and earth streams into you."

It is important to understand that it is possible for every person to be successful at work. Elbert Hubbard puts it emphatically: "Success is the most natural thing in the world. The person who does not succeed has placed himself in opposition to the laws of the Universe." In other words, the only one who can keep you from succeeding is you by blocking your own creative flow. You are not a helpless creature adrift on the seas of life, trying desperately to make something of yourself against impossible odds. The creative intention is vitally involved in you. Thus your desire to get ahead, your urge to succeed, is your intuitive awareness of something within you that wants to succeed through you.

There is another side of this relentless drive for success. We will call it the "Success Syndrome." It is a factor that is at once the key to success and the reason for much failure. The success urge is basic in the American dream.

Here anyone can be on top of the heap, so most people want to be—or feel guilty because they think they _should_ want to be. People holding the same job assignment for years may be asked, "Are you still on that job?" The implication is, "Why haven't you progressed?" Actually, they are happy and fulfilled in what to them is a perfectly stimulating work. Progression is not measured alone by the title on the office door. More important is what people have done with themselves. When viewed through the Success Syndrome, people should be dissatisfied with their work. Many people are influenced by this pressure, thus are unable to put their full effort into their work, feeling that they should be climbing, prospering, succeeding. Instead of earning their wings every day, they yearn for bigger airplanes. It is a drive that is basic to humankind, but unfortunately, instead of seeing it as a cosmic urge to _be_ more, it is normally interpreted as the desire to _have_ more.

Under the Success Syndrome, we are conditioned to feel that _we_ must always be getting ahead and there can be no rest until we reach the top. And because the pyramid narrows on the way upward, there simply is not room for everyone in the highest echelons of business. Thus most persons harbor a secret sense of failure. They may have fine jobs with ample incomes and live in lovely homes, and yet even an assistant manager or a vice president hasn't reached the top post. Thus there may be an inner feeling of frustration.

It is interesting to note how we are conditioned to this

feeling in our formative years. Children in school are under tremendous pressure from their parents to get good grades. It is made clear that getting an "A" or "B" is more important than learning itself. A "C" grade, supposed to be satisfactory, is considered, in effect, a failure, a cause of shame. So children who may need to gain more from education than right answers and whose curiosity may lead them to ask uncomfortable questions are marked down in grades. They just don't fit into a system that is geared toward the Success Syndrome. We tend, thus, to stigmatize them with a self-image of failure that will remain with them through all their lives.

People who have been conditioned under the Success Syndrome tend to consider success always in terms of the grades, the salaries, the nameplate on the office door, the titles—getting there is all that counts. A common symptom of this conditioning is the wandering eye, where people are forever looking at better jobs while purportedly engaged in their own. They jump from job to job in their attempt to achieve the top. However, even if they arrive at the high levels of business, they may have so overemphasized the goal of *getting there* that their inner growth, the organic flow, may not have been cultivated. In other words, they succeed in getting there but they are not really convinced of their right to be there.

And when we set such a high premium upon getting there and on the high standard of living that defines the field in which "there" exists, little wonder so many persons become almost paranoid in the desire to protect it. The standard *of* living becomes more important than any standard *for* living and the end of reaching the top and staying there may justify any means needed, at the expense of the ethical, the moral, or even the legal.

In recent years this drive for the success of getting there has given rise to courses in success-motivation and self-image psychology and many others, offering surefire techniques for achieving the top. All of them contain some helpful insights, but when dealt with in the narrow focus of getting there at any cost, they may be dangerously self-deluding. Michael Korda, in his book *Success!* says that a high level of Machiavellian behavior is a necessary ingredient for success. In other words, you must be devious if you want to succeed. Robert Ringer gives much the same message in his best-selling books, *Looking Out for Number One* and *Winning Through Intimidation*. Books of this type have found an eager market among people who are lost in the world of materialism and mercilessly driven by the Success Syndrome.

Success is not getting there; it is earning the right in consciousness to be there. Two persons may arrive at successful positions at the top of their field. One has clawed his or her way up and continues to fearfully hold on for dear life because within, he or she is not sure of belonging there. The other is there because he or she has earned his or her wings every day. By appearances, you cannot really know the difference.

Perhaps we need a new model of success, where the "good life" refers more to "values" than to "valuables." We might do well to reconsider the kind of idealism expressed on a tombstone in Boston Commons: "Here lies the body of Andrew Murray who cobbled shoes to the glory of God for 40 years."

This is not to advocate a retreat from the kind of drive that has set America apart as a nation of achievers and strivers for affluence. It is simply to suggest that we need to consider recapturing the pioneering emphasis on the essential worth of the person. Have we really made a success of our lives unless we have expanded the awareness of ourselves in the process? Is success simply a corporate grade or should we consider it on the basis of growth that is taking place within the person? It may not be an acceptable standard for the marketplace, but if you are serious about prospering through spiritual economics, then it should be an acceptable standard for you. Of course, you can succeed in your work, you can reach the top and become the best, without limits. Just be certain that it comes out of the *expanse* of your inner growth and not at its *expense*. Only you can know, but very definitely, *you know!*

Remember, consciousness is the key. Make a new commitment to think of your work not as a place to make a living but as an opportunity to make a life. Think of yourself as a channel through which creative activities flow, and there is no limit. Your mind is one with the same mind that is in the genius, the successful, and the affluent. Wonderful ideas and boundless energies flow forth easily through you, making you indispensable and appreciated in your work. You are free from tension or stress, for you know that you are an inlet and may become an outlet to all there is in God. You are not alone. The whole Universe is on your side, guiding your hands and directing your footsteps in the way you go. A helpful affirmation is: _I am God's living enterprise, and God cannot fail._ There can be no failure in God. Any appearance of failure is in consciousness, a frustration of the creative potential. No matter what your job or your chosen career, your true business is the "express business," the business of releasing your imprisoned splendor. Infinite Mind will always regulate your affairs so that you have an adequate job in which to "sing your song" or express your potential. If the job becomes inadequate, if you keep yourself in tune with the creative flow, either the job will change or you will be moved to another job. Nothing can impede the flow of affluence and success to one who keeps one's self in tune. Remember: _I am God's living enterprise, and God cannot fail._

CHAPTER 7

How to Reverse Financial Adversity

I t is sometimes said of a person that one is "into the market." Usually, this indicates that the person has an investment portfolio of stocks and bonds. In a very real sense, we are all "into the market," for unless we are living as a hermit in a cave, we require goods and services in order to live and a source of income to make it possible, which is very much affected by the fluctuation of the economy.

It is being increasingly acknowledged that economics is basically a psychological phenomenon. Government agencies may release statistics and charts indicating fluctuations of the workforce, business activity, interest rates, and the gross national product. Very impressive! Conveniently, nothing is said about the cause. This is because it is a mystical process, dealing with the trends of the thoughts of "we, the people." The "economy" as far as we are concerned will always be to us about what we make it, how we decree it, what we expect it to be.

In the conversations at the bridge table, during coffee breaks, and just about everywhere people pass the time of day, the major items of discussion are job security, the deficit, interest rates, the erosion of the value of the dollar, and the price of food at the supermarket. If the consensus is that "something awful is happening," then something *is* happening right there. For the economy is little more than a barometer that registers the highs and lows of conscious-ness. Wherever two or three are gathered together in an interaction of minds, a very real energy force is projected into the world. If it happens to be a prayer group or a positive discussion group, then there is a healing or prosperity influence. If it is the sharing of negativity, as is so often the case, that consciousness goes forth as a beacon of darkness, adding to the weakening of the economy. Many analysts have searched for causes for the fluctuations of the stock market. Perhaps they need look no further than here.

There was an article on the front page of the *Wall Street Journal* some years ago that said, "Positive thinking is the way out of our economic malaise." It went on to decry the excessive pessimism that is now engulfing us. It quoted the president of a large corporation as urging business leaders to adopt a more positive attitude to help dispel fears of impending economic doom and to restore confidence in the American people. It is easy to let such advice go right over our heads just agreeing, "Yes, that is something 'they' should do." However, you are the leader of your business affairs. And, as a student of Truth, you should become a leader in all conversational groupings. Thus whenever the discussion turns to the high cost of things and the lagging business of your employer and the frightening cycles of inflation and recession, don't acquiesce in negative conclusions. Position yourself squarely on the side of the prosperity potential and "let something good be said." People may be talking about supply-side economics; perhaps what is needed is Truth-side economics.

Psalm 1:1–3 has a great prosperity lesson for contemporary times:

> "Blessed is the man
> who walks not in the counsel of the wicked,
> nor stands in the way of sinners,
> nor sits in the seat of scoffers;
> but his delight is in the law of the Lord,
> and on his law he meditates day and night.
> He is like a tree
> planted by streams of water,
> that yields its fruit in its season,
> and its leaf does not wither.
> In all that he does, he prospers."

The Psalmist clearly states that if you refuse to agree with the gossip of negative people (the council of the wicked) and keep yourself in tune with the divine law of prosperity, then you can be certain that substance will flow as easily to you as substance flows to the tree planted by the river of water. A very important realization!

The great discovery of the new insight in Truth is that consciousness is the key to all things which happen to us, certainly the key to personal prosperity. The starting point in changing your life from financial reverses to an experience of abundance is the realization that you can change your life by altering your thoughts. You begin by taking responsibility for your own life. As long as you are hung up on paranoid thoughts such as "It is what they are doing," "It is what is happening in Washington," "Office politics!" and "The IRS is harassing me," then you cannot find help of any kind through Truth.

Admit to yourself that your present experience, even the condition of your bank account, reflects your present level of awareness. You are not the victim of circumstances. Consciousness creates circumstances or at least sets the climate in which they happen. When you establish yourself in this awareness, then you are in a position to change things. Because if the cause is in you, in your level of consciousness, then the cure can be affected by changing your thoughts, by altering the cause. If, however, the cause is "out there" in people or circumstances, then there is little you can do. "It's just one of those things." Again, the need is not to find the way to get something but to alter the inner states of mind that have been blocking the natural flow of substance in your life. It may be reflected in a salary increase, or it could result in some investment dividends; essentially it will come through consciousness.

Now we live in a world of many crosscurrents of consciousness. If we are honest, we will admit that we are not always able to sustain positive attitudes in all circumstances. Negativity sometimes floods the mind and there seems little we can do about it. Thus, for one reason or another, things sometimes go wrong. Perhaps it is a job that hasn't worked out, maybe it is a sudden need for financing in a tight money market or an unexpected loss in a heavily depended-on investment.

In every attempt in life, there must be the possibility of success *and* failure. We must have the stability and the perspective to deal with both success and failure in spiritual poise. You see, to become too elated with success and too crushed by defeat is indicative of an imbalance. In every setback, we should be buoyed up with the realization that nothing is ever a complete loss. There is always some gain, some growth. And in every success, we should be humbled with the realization that without the action of forces greater than ourselves, we could not have succeeded.

Life is fundamentally a matter of growing, a growth experience. Missing the mark is one of the ways in which we learn to hit the target. Failure is a vital part of achieving success. We have erroneously thought of success as "getting there," while *actually* success is "earning the right to be there." And earning means learning. Setbacks, even failures, may be an important part of that learning. This may include a stock that didn't perform as expected, a brief fling in a business that failed, or even an occasional experience of unemployment. They are all ways in which we earn the right to achieve the prosperity and success that we all dream about.

Any education that prepares people only for success and not for coping with the frustration of things going wrong is sadly deficient. It simply succeeds in inhibiting a large number of people from attempting ventures where failure is a possibility, which severely cripples this creativity and imagination.

One of the most challenging reverses that we ever have to deal with is unemployment. The important thing is, it is not being unemployed or even being employed that makes the difference in our lives but how we accept these conditions—the attitudes, the feelings, the general tone of our consciousness—as we face the experience. There are some employed people who live in constant fear of being laid off. And there are people out of work who have complete confidence that it is a transition which will lead inevitably to betterment. The people who have jobs and are constantly afraid they will be dismissed are already blocking their flow. They are setting a time bomb that will go off at some future time—perhaps not in the actual loss of their jobs, but in some frustration in the job or in some kind of financial stringency.

The sad thing is that many persons who are unemployed have actually become unemployable because they have allowed the idea of lack and inactivity to become established in their consciousness. Unemployment and the self-pity and bitterness associated with it become an obsession that blocks the activity of re-employment or the re-infusion of the substance flow. The first need is not to find a job but to change the self-image, to resign from enlistment in the "army of the unemployed." Don't see yourself as unemployed but as "ready for work." As long as you are "unemployed," you will tend to identify with the Labor Department statistics showing things to be so bad that it might even be foolish to look for work. However, if you are "ready for work," you are in an entirely different ball game.

If you should be out of work, then you really have a job, the most important and challenging job you have ever had. The job is to get work. Set about this job as you would any other job. Get up early, pack your lunch, get neatly dressed, and set off enthusiastically and expectantly in your work of finding a job. The important thing: work at it. See it as a challenge to your faith and determine to grow through the experience. Don't listen to the advice of the crepe-hangers (what Psalm 1 calls "the council of the wicked"). They will be singing their perpetual dirge: "No jobs to be had," "Recession is inevitable," "At your age," and so on.

You are a whole person in a whole Universe. You are an

individualized expression of the creative flow. There is something you can do that no one can do quite as uniquely as you. Somewhere there is a need for that special contribution. You are needed even as you have a need. If you lose sight of this awareness, you abdicate from the Universe. As you sit thinking, "If I could only find a job," some employer is at that very moment thinking, "If only we could locate the right person for this opening!" Keep that vision of the orderly Universe. It is not a miracle that is needed to create a job for you but an expression of divine order in bringing you together with that which is looking for you.

There is a Divine Mind counterpart for every human need. There is an answer for every problem, substance for every financial requirement, a job for every willing worker. The economic indicators will not tell you this. The welfare agencies will not tell you this. You will need to tell it to yourself, for economics is a spiritual process. As far as your experience in the marketplace is concerned, you make the difference!

There is an innocuous phrase used often in the Bible: "It came to pass." It has a subtle inference that can be extremely meaningful to you. The problem or financial reversal did not come into your life to stay; it came to pass. Whatever the challenge, refuse to be panic-stricken. Life hasn't ended for you. It flows on in a healing and prospering stream. In the face of any challenge, affirm: *I accept the reality of this situation, but not its permanence.* The experience is there to be met. There is no use hiding your head in the sand. However, determine to meet it on your terms. Don't let the outer happening squeeze you into its box, but open your mind to the flow of wisdom and love and good judgment with which you can deal masterfully with it. It has come to pass. Accept it, but accept it as a changing experience that is on its way out. Something better is on the way for you.

For instance, in meeting the experience of unemployment, normally there is fear, self-pity, and a sense of insecurity. It is important to understand that this comes from a subtle acceptance of the permanence of the condition. If you hold to the thought that it has come to pass, seeing it as a moving experience, suddenly your confidence is restored, along with your feeling of oneness with the divine flow.

In the study of Truth, we talk often about the power of words. It is important to put into verbal form only those statements that you really want to see manifest in your life. Certainly, we are all too permissive in the things that we say about financial conditions in the world. Sometimes the difficulty is in the repeated use of words that could be replaced with some which have a more positive suggestion. For instance, the word *problem*. You may say, "I have this problem." Immediately the mind turns to dark meanings and impassable obstacles and impossible people. A much better word to employ when referring to some kind of challenge is *project*. Note what happens when you say, "I have this 'project.'" It makes all the difference in the world. The word *project* suggests a positive endeavor of development. There is a tendency to deal with a problem with tension and strain and the "only a miracle can save me now" consciousness. We tackle a project such as putting a man on the moon with vigor and imagination and in the conviction that it will be done.

What projects do you have before you in your life? If you make a list of problems, you might well wring your hands and feel terrible about your burden. But a list of projects! It even has an exciting ring. Can't you just see yourself rubbing your hands in enthusiasm, eager to commence, and expectant of a positive outworking?

Take a careful look at the challenges you are facing: a possible layoff, an important career decision, the inability to make ends meet on your current income. If you identify these as your "problems," there is a tendency to see them as static and burdensome and with a feeling of resentment and self-pity. And in the quest for solutions, you will invariably be looking for help or advice from people or for some "miracle of God." In other words, you are looking for someone, even God, to shoulder the responsibility. But it simply won't work! However, see the challenges as "projects," and you tune in on a whole different flow of consciousness. You are faced with some opportunities to grow, but you feel secure in the awareness that, in the main, the answers will unfold from within. There is a sense of lightness, of clear horizons, and of confident expectancy. It is the same so-called "trouble," but your attitude is different. And according to your thoughts, your faith, and your feeling, it will be done unto you. It is a mystic teaching that is ages old but amazingly relevant.

Whenever you are faced with a knotty financial dilemma, you always have a clear choice of how you will deal with it. If you brood over the letdown, the disappointment in a job, or some complete collapse of a financial involvement, you simply magnify it out of all proportion. It is like taking a pebble off the beach and holding it close to your eyes. It may be a small stone, but held close enough it can completely screen your view. Hold it at a proper viewing distance and it can be examined and properly dealt with. Drop it at your feet and it can become a part of a stone path. The Psalmist says, "Thou hast put all things under his [humankind's] feet" (Ps. 8:6 KJV).

The loss of a job or the failure of some important financial project, held too closely in consciousness, may appear to be the end of everthing. As one man said when he was passed over for promotion to a higher position: "My life is over! I just can't go on." And because he allowed this experience to obscure all else, he brooded for months and became so lethargic in his work that he very nearly lost the position he did have. Fortunately, in time, he came to his senses, realizing that by reason of his immature reaction, he proved his unworthiness for the greater responsibility. Life did go on. And later he was picked for a higher post much more suited to his creative abilities. So it proved to be a growth experience.

It has been said that there is a little paranoia in everyone. Thus when some untoward thing occurs, it is not at all unusual for us to react in a way that implies that the Universe is picking on us. Why did this happen to me? How could "they" do this? One man said of his company that laid him off after twenty years of employment, "They ruined my life and completely made a bum out of me." Can't you just see him walking down the railroad tracks carrying his possessions in a red bandana tied to the end of a stick over his shoulder? Poor man! They ruined his life! Of course it is total delusion. No one can ruin your life. You are always responsible for the way you accept the things that happen to you. The incident is external; the reaction is always your own. A financial crisis may have occurred, and it may appear that you are at the bottom financially, but it is still "out there." You are still an inlet and may become an outlet to all there is in God. You may have been fired from your job, but no one can ever fire you from the Universe! You are still God's living enterprise, and God cannot fail.

All that really counts is what is happening within you. How are you reacting to the experience? Where is your faith? Within you is a limitless, unborn potential of creativity and substance, and the present experience can be your great opportunity to give birth to it. Thus, if you will, the tragedy can become a blessing, the disadvantage can become an advantage, the failure can become an opportunity, and the disappointment can become "God's" appointment.

When you are grounded in the field of limitless substance, then you may be broke, but you can never be poor. It is a marvelous awareness to hold to. You live in the wisdom and substance of Infinite Mind. You may be out of work, but you cannot be out of the flow of creativity. You may have a difficulty, but you are forever one with the guiding light of Spirit by which you can go through the experience, and even grow through it. Shakespeare had this in mind when he said in *As You Like It:*

Sweet are the uses of adversity,
Which, like the toad, ugly and venomous,
Wears yet a precious Jewel in its head;
And this our life, exempt from public haunt,
Finds tongues in trees, books in the running brooks,
Sermons in stones, and good in everything.

You can learn a helpful lesson from the lowly oyster. He is normally a very placid fellow, but occasionally little grains of sand work their way inside his shell and begin irritating him. Naturally, he tries to get rid of them. But when he discovers he can't do this, he settles down and produces one of the most priceless and beautiful things in the world. He turns the irritation into a pearl. So, no matter what the difficulty, the loss, the financial adversity; if you are feeling negative, get busy pearling.

By the "all things work together for good" principle, any experience of life can become the best thing that ever happened to you. Haven't you said or heard someone say, "I was certainly upset about that challenge, but now as I see it in retrospect, it was the best possible thing that could have happened"? It is occasionally said of alcoholism, drug addiction, bankruptcy, or unemployment. But why wait? Why not accept the possibility right when the crisis occurs?

Why not pick out the most difficult thing facing you right now and say: *I know that this is the best thing that could happen to me, for I know that in the happening there is revealed a new lesson to learn and some new growth to experience. I know that within me is an unborn possibility of limitless potentialities, and this is my opportunity to begin to give birth to new ideas, new strength, and new vision. I accept the reality of the difficulty but not its permanence. I am not at the end of anything. I am simply between opportunities, between jobs. I know that in the movement of "it has come to pass," something wonderful is on its way to me far surpassing anything I have ever known before. And if I should feel the slightest irritation of fear or anxiety, I will say to myself, "All right, let's get busy pearling."*

Security in a Changing World

Security is one of the most talked about things in the world today. Every day in the news reports there are discussions of how nations are going about the business of securing themselves. Families plan for security by putting bars on the windows and locks on the doors. Individuals give a lot of attention to such things as insurance of various kinds, investing in stocks and bonds, contributing to "nest egg" savings programs, and retirement annuities. Everyone longs for the feeling expressed by the Psalmist: "My heart is fixed, O God, my heart is fixed: I will sing and give praise" (Ps. 57:7 KJV).

Is this kind of security possible? If so, how do we achieve it? It depends upon what we think that security is. If we are thinking of security in terms of protective barriers and a continuous provision for food, clothing, shelter, heat, light, and medical care, then (and this may seem shocking) the most secure individual is a life-term convict in a penitentiary. Almost everything is cared for, thus he or she has little to worry about. He or she has real security, but at such a great price!

Most public opinion surveys indicate that the one thing most people desire in life more than anything else is security. This is a sad commentary on contemporary values. Professor Peter Bartocci of Boston University has said, "It may be that any view of life that puts security rather than creativity first has misread life at its best, and thus misinterprets the cosmic process." This is not to suggest that the desire for security is wrong or that we shouldn't seek ways of achieving it. It is simply that when we place the emphasis on outer things, we miss the whole meaning of life. Life is for expressing, for growth and expansion.

There are two basic drives within every person: human and divine. Humanly, we seek to settle down, to be safe, to build fences, and to be secure. Divinely, we are created to express, to grow, and to extend our horizons. If we had not risen above the human inclination to be safe at all costs, we would still be living in caves, if indeed the human race would still be living at all.

In the early days of life on Earth, Homo sapiens were surrounded by great beasts with superb built-in defenses: tusks, hides, claws, wings, shells, and tremendous brute strength. The human creatures, seemingly so inadequate, so helpless, survived because their defense was in their creative ability, in the intuitive flow of ideas, in their spiritual dimension—no matter how primitive was its showing.

If humankind had always tried simply to be safe at all costs, there would have been no Moses leaving the comfort of Egypt to lead his people through a vast wilderness and into their Promised Land. There would have been no Columbus braving uncharted seas to discover a new world. When people think only of being safe, they stifle the urges of personal growth and advancement.

People in the study of Truth often enroll in courses on "How to Demonstrate Affluence" and even "How to Become a Millionaire." Unfortunately, the appeal is geared to the "acquisitive instinct." What the writers and teachers who talk so glibly of the "millionaire consciousness" tend to conveniently overlook is that the millionaire models they use, to a person, achieved their great affluence, not because of a desire to find security, but because they were entrepreneurs, risk-takers, and adventurers who launched out beyond the barriers of accepted limitations. Someone has said (and it could well have been one of these models) that the best way to be safe is never to be secure.

What are we saying? That we should not take out insurance or save or invest our money? Not at all! Actually, security is more psychological than financial. Feeling is the key! Whatever financial measures we take, if we are motivated by fear or anxiety, then we mine our roadway into the future with booby traps. But if we plan and conserve and keep our thoughts centered in God as our limitless resource of good, then our way will be filled with success and fulfillment. It depends on what we are thinking when we do what we do. As the Bible says, "Except the Lord build the house, they labour in vain that build it" (Ps. 127:1 KJV).

As a student of Truth, you may have been perplexed about the matter of insurance. When the emphasis is normally on divine protection and "stepping out on the promises" in faith, it would seem to be a kind of backsliding to take out policies for life or fire or economic assistance. The salesperson may outline to you all the cataclysmic things that could happen to you, and of course, for which he or she would like to insure you. You may be confused between the very practical matter of financial protection and the idea of trusting in the divine process.

Let's face it, there is no such thing as complete insurance coverage. Highly insecure people, trying to prepare for every conceivable exigency, become "insurance poor" in the attempt. If you have this kind of anxiety, this unbridled fear of anything and everything that might happen down the road, then you need insurance, and you need it badly. Why? Because the conditions you fear will probably happen. It is a universal law that the patterns you hold in mind tend to influence circumstances.

Living in an insurance-conscious culture, it may be

wise to have at least minimal insurance coverage in the major areas of life. This, because we tend to absorb from the race consciousness, as by osmosis, the kind of thought patterns posed by insurance people. Jesus, in referring to the tax liability, said, "Render therefore unto Caesar the things which are Caesar's; and unto God the things that are God's" (Mt. 22:21 KJV). It is good to start off on an automobile trip with four good tires and a spare tire so you can relax and enjoy the journey. The spare tire is not a symbol of fear but rather an evidence of wisdom and good planning.

Now, people may insist that they put their trust in God and in no other agency and that they do not need and will not accept insurance. And other than automobile insurance, which may be required in some states, we bless them in their stand. However, a word of caution. There is a great difference between *wanting* to believe and *really* believing. Recall the honesty of the man who asked Jesus for help: "I believe; help my unbelief!" (Mk. 9:24) All too often people refuse to face up to their hidden unbelief and willfully follow a self-delusive course of independence. Not accepting responsibility for their affairs and without the consciousness of divine protection, they leave their health care or financial welfare to others or to society, which is a kind of irresponsible behavior. In practical matters, it is wise to listen to your consciousness and not just to your ideals. Often someone will ask, "Should I have an operation as prescribed by my doctor or should I trust in God to heal me?" It is a puzzling question to which we offer a startling answer. God doesn't heal! God is life. Consciousness heals as it accepts the flow of life. If you have a deep-seated fear about your condition, it is not likely that you will be able to accept the healing life flow. Lacking in the consciousness of oneness with the ever-present activity of God, you might be well advised to follow your doctor's guidance. Again, listen to your consciousness. Let no one decide for you whether or not you should have an operation. It is your life, governed by your state of mind. If you really believe, then press on with the courage of your convictions. However, don't delude yourself. If there are fears or anxious concerns, then you have unbelief, and you should consider following some physical course of action.

The same holds true in the matter of insurance. God will protect, of course. Actually, God is a protecting force which is ever present. You live and move and have being under this *shadow of the Almighty*. It is present, all-present, as a Presence. You can never be outside its influence. If you can live in the consciousness of this Presence, you literally take on a protective mantle, and nothing untoward can happen around you or to you. However, if you are not centered in that consciousness, or at least are not able to long sustain it, then perhaps it is wise to take the "spare tire," thus to employ some minimal kind of insurance. Then you can relax and let go and have faith. Again, let no one tell you what you should do.

Listen to your consciousness honestly and follow its leading courageously.

How should one consider investments in planning for financial security? Investments are a wise use of one's resources. Even as it is important that you engage in some form of work, so it is also wise to let your money work too. Again, motivation is the key. Why do you want to invest your money? If you are gambling or "trying to make a killing on the stock market," you are trying to take a shortcut to wealth and security, which inevitably will be self-defeating.

Whatever you do in the way of investments, do it out of the consciousness of the divine flow. Keep yourself centered in God so that you do not flutter like a flag in the breeze when the Dow Jones report is published every day. Keep your faith in the continuity of God's ever-present substance, no matter what the condition of the market in general or your stock in particular. You might use this affirmation: *I give thanks to God as the source of my supply, and I bless (name your investment) as a channel through which it may manifest.*

Students also ask questions about saving. Isn't the practice negative? Why should I save if I am a child of God, supported by the Universe like the lily of the field? Once again, it is the motivation that is the key. If you save for a "rainy day," then it will undoubtedly rain buckets, and often. Job discovered a great Truth as he admitted that "the thing that I fear comes upon me" (Job 3:25).

Why do you feel that you should save? Is it because you are afraid of tomorrow? Is it because you doubt the sufficiency of the ever-present substance of the Universe? Actually, saving is a mature practice. All nature saves. The physical body is a self-conserving process. Note how the great lakes of the world conserve water to sustain the Earth's flora all the year around. So we can see that saving is natural, and it is orderly. However, get the high vision: save for opportunities, not for emergencies.

You may continue to do what you have been doing, but with a new attitude. Let your savings program be a divinely ordered process. Even as a bank or other agency keeps watch over your funds, it is your responsibility to keep watch over your thoughts. If you commence or continue in any program out of the thought that "this nest egg will tide me over if something should happen," then you are engaging in it in an emergency consciousness. You may actually be creating an environment in which such things can happen. Save, by all means. It will enable you to avail yourself of positive opportunities that may, from time to time, unfold. Again, save not for emergencies but for opportunities.

However, it is important that you clearly understand this: you can't get a prosperity consciousness on the stock market. You can't achieve true security through insurance. And you won't get rich simply by saving your money. But if you work diligently to establish yourself in the consciousness of the divine flow of substance, actually get the feeling that you live in the boundless sea of affluence, then by the steadying and supportive influence of this consciousness, your assets may surely grow through investment, your affairs may be cared for by insurance, and your wisely planned savings may become a vehicle for prosperity. But remember the "rich mentality" will not come because of your financial involvements. It must come first out of your steady effort to know God as your supply. "Seek first his kingdom" (Mt. 6:33). Seek first to get the awareness of the Allness of substance. Out of that awareness, you will *feel* secure. This feeling will give rise to the ideas and the guidance by which you invest your money or decide on insurance, and so on. But you do what you do out of a consciousness of security.

Now, a few thoughts about retirement programs and annuities. Along with the government provision for the IRA (Individual Retirement Account), there is much talk about the need for some form of retirement program. Much of it presents the negative image of old age and the out-to-pasture kind of uselessness. Get out of the retirement business! Not that you shouldn't make changes in your lifework and your lifestyle. By all means plan for changes and for new beginnings. However, always think "creativity and involvement." Never let yourself get in a position where you are "out of it." Don't fall into the sunbelt-condominium syndrome. You can't live meaningfully and creatively on a shuffleboard court.

In a recent study of centenarians, it was discovered

that there was not one retired-to-do-nothing person who lived to be a hundred. You may say that you are not concerned about living to be a hundred. Perhaps not! But are you interested in remaining alive and vital as long as you live? The life change of retirement may be good for you, but only if it is seen not as an end but as a redirection of activities and interests.

One must work diligently at the continuing process of keeping the whole self alive and fully functioning. The Truth is, we do not *grow* old; when we stop growing, we *are* old.

One man was cleaning up his work at his desk on a Friday evening when he noticed an envelope that had not been opened. Apparently it had been placed there while he was on the telephone. He opened it and read, to his shock and dismay, a notice of termination. His entire department was being eliminated and his position along with it. After all the years he had given to this corporation, he found himself filled with resentment and a sense of injustice.

Long past his planned time of departure, the man sat slumped in his chair in utter despair and defeat. It has been said that the experience of retirement is the greatest shock the system can sustain. He thought through all the terrible things that could happen to him: he would have to sell his house and alter his whole way of life. He was not really prepared financially for retirement, and yet he was at an age normally considered too old to get another job. The specter of lack, poverty, and destitution hovered on the horizon. Even more severe was the shock of feeling that he was no longer needed—useless, through, washed up.

He noticed a spider on the desk, and he unconsciously brushed it off. Suddenly, he was watching in amazement as the tiny creature automatically spun a strand to bear its weight and swung gracefully to the floor. He began to wonder: Why, if this tiny creature could draw forth from within itself a reserve of substance to meet its emergency, why could he not do as much? For many hours, he sat deep in troubled thoughts that turned gradually to creative meditation.

Finally, the conviction came that the source of his supply, his security, was not in jobs or money or houses or lands, but in his oneness with the Allness of Infinite Mind. He might be taken from a payroll, but no one could cut him off from the intuitive flow of his own mind. This, he realized, was his real lifeline.

This man was of an artistic nature. Being forced to do office work had always irked him. Figuratively, he had been earning his livelihood by the sweat of his brow, in his spare time, he had done a little writing which occasionally found publication. He had secretly longed for the opportunity to write for a living. Now, he realized, was that opportunity. So a whole new frame of mind took possession of him. He blessed his retirement and thanked God for the new door that had opened before him. He left the office with a buoyancy and confidence that surprised even himself.

It would be good to report that the man went on to great success as a writer. Real life isn't made up of great success and great failure but of an infinite number of levels of living in between. And true greatness depends more on inner overcomings than on outer achievements. Our man did accomplish some great things within himself. He gained a new sense of self-mastery, a new sense of satisfaction and happiness, and he did enough good writing to earn a few checks each month—enough to more than double his half-pay retirement income.

The word *secure* comes from two small Latin words: *se* meaning "without" and *cure* meaning "care"—being without care, freedom from anxiety. Victor Hugo articulates this very special sense in this lovely couplet:

> Be like the bird
> That pausing in her flight
> While on boughs too slight,
> Feels them give way
> Beneath her, and yet sings,
> Knowing she hath wings.

You may be surrounded by grim forebodings of job layoffs and of deficit and of the sure failure of the social security system. How good it is to remind yourself often that your security is not in "boughs too slight" but in your wings of faith, your intuitive relationship with the divine process which flows from within. In a changing world, you may not be able to keep difficulties from happening around you. You can't control the stock market or what happens to the dollar. Occasionally, figuratively speaking, you might even be in water over your head. But if you can swim, the deep water is not all that bad, is it? What is swimming but fun, if you are not afraid of the water?

In his immortal Sermon on the Mount (Mt. 6:25–34), Jesus gives a timeless formula for security. You might profit immeasurably by meditating on these words every day:

"Do not be anxious about your life, what you shall eat or what you shall drink, nor about your body, what you shall put on. Is not life more than food, and the body more than clothing? Look at the birds of the air: they neither sow nor reap nor gather into barns, and yet your heavenly Father feeds them. Are you not of more value than they? And which of you by being anxious can add one cubit to his span of life? And why are you anxious about clothing? Consider the lilies of the field, how they grow; they neither toil nor spin; yet I tell you, even Solomon in all his glory was not arrayed like one of these. But if God so clothes the grass of the field, which today is alive and tomorrow is thrown into the oven, will he not much more clothe you, O men of little faith? There-

fore do not be anxious, saying, 'What shall we eat?'
or 'What shall we drink?' or 'What shall we wear?'
For the Gentiles seek all these things; and your
heavenly Father knows that you need them all. But
seek first his kingdom and his righteousness, and all
these things shall be yours as well. Therefore do not
be anxious about tomorrow, for tomorrow will be
anxious for itself. Let the day's own trouble be sufficient for the day."

To reiterate, security is not found in things. You are not
secure because of a bank account. You are not secure because of your investments or your possessions. Security
can be experienced in one way only—by identifying
yourself as a channel for the flow of Infinite Mind. Ideas
are the gold coin of the kingdom, literally little chunks of
divine substance, out of which we mold and fashion our
good. Money may be depleted, things may wear out or be
lost or stolen, but ideas endure and re-create. And when
you have the great idea in mind that you are an individualized expression of the universal flow, then truly, as
Thoreau says, "You may live with the license of a higher
order of beings." When you know this, really know it,
then no matter how prices go up and stocks go down, no
matter how rampant over the media are the rumors of recession and inflation and layoffs and shortages, you will
not be affected.

Antoinette Bourignon made a great stir in the religious

life of seventeenth-century France. When she was eighteen years old, she resolved to give her life to God. Her family tried to dissuade her and finally attempted to force her into an unwelcome marriage. One morning, prompted by an inner voice, Antoinette ran away, taking with her nothing but one penny for bread. As she left, she heard a voice within saying, "Where is your faith? In a penny?" She reflected a moment, then laid it aside saying, "No, Lord, my faith is in Thee and in Thee alone." William James comments on this in his *Varieties of Religious Experience:* "That penny was a small financial safeguard, but an effective spiritual obstacle."

Where is your faith? Search yourself honestly. Is your faith in your "penny": your bank account, your job, your insurance, your retirement annuities? You may say, "But one must be practical!" Of course! But what are you really building your life upon? Can you take the rich-young-ruler test? Do you remember that young man of means who wanted to be a disciple? Jesus told him to go sell all he had and give the money to the poor, and then he could come and follow him. Jesus wasn't saying that we should not have money. What he was testing for was to determine if the man had possessions or if he was possessed by them. That the young man "turned sorrowfully away" would indicate that the latter was the case.

Are you willing to test yourself? Close your eyes and imagine everything of value being swept away, leaving you completely destitute. Are you gripped with a cold fear? Now, where is your faith? It is a shocking test of consciousness, pinpointing the difference between your net worth and your net worthiness. You will invariably be anxious about what you are worth but completely at peace over what you are worthy of. In the Hebrew, the word for security is a word that literally means "worthy." True security is in worthiness, not in worth. If you are completely locked in to your money and possessions, your net worth, you may well be unconsciously trying to cover your unworthiness. And the more security you require to cover your unworthiness, the more you feel insecure. Thus despite properties, stock portfolio, and a good income, you live almost frantically attuned to the economic indicators, all because you have a secret sense of unworthiness. If you really feel worthy, you can let it all go and put the whole weight of your faith on the everlasting arms. If you find a deficiency through this test, you can do something about it, and you should. Study Chapter 1 again, working diligently to build a consciousness of God as substance in which you live and move and have being.

Here is an affirmation treatment that is intended as a work assignment for this lesson. Speak it aloud, going through it several times until you feel that you have grasped its essence in your consciousness. And, finally, close your eyes and let the Truth of the words sink into your inmost and deeper-than-conscious level of mind:

I am secure, for I know who I am: a richly endowed child

of God. I am secure in all I do, for I know my oneness with the divine process. I am secure in all I have, for I know my treasure is in my mind, not in my things. I live my life from day to day as if God's supportive substance were as exhaustless and dependable as the air I breathe, which it most certainly is.

CHAPTER 9

The Money Enigma

There is little likelihood that your life can become fully functioning with prosperity unless you have a positive and creative attitude toward money. It is rare that a day will pass when you will not have some kind of monetary involvement with the world. You may go into the day with the highest intention to walk in the light of Truth. But if you have not resolved the "money enigma," you quickly lose your lofty awareness the moment you dip into your wallet.

A survey was once conducted by a research department of the University of Michigan. In essence, they wanted to know what effect money had on the lives of people. Three of their findings:

What do people worry about most?
Money!

What makes people the happiest? Money!
What makes people the unhappiest? Money!

You may say these results do not include you, for your
mind is stayed on God as ever-present substance. But no
matter how lofty your spiritual ideals may be, no matter
how many powerful affirmations of Truth you can speak
by rote, you still have to pay your bills. Emerson obviously
experienced difficulties with this. He tells of a man who
"rose to the empyrean heights and dove to the unfath-
omable depths, but never paid cash."

This chapter is included in the prosperity study full
well realizing that there are some persons who think it is
a sacrilege to talk about money in a spiritual context.
They are quick to quote Scripture: Money is the root of all
evils. Actually, this is the most misquoted of all Bible pas-
sages. What Paul really said is, "The love of money is the
root of all evils" (1 Tim. 6:10). Money is innocent. It is the
love of money, the consciousness in which you use money,
that is the cause of much limitation. And you could turn
it around and say, "The right attitude toward money is a
root of all kinds of prosperity."

It is just such misquotation of the Bible (there are
many other instances) that has given rise to the confused
dualism about money in the religions of the Western
world. On the one hand, riches have been condemned as
dangerous to man's spiritual growth, while on the other
hand, churches have needed money for their support and

have welcomed the affluent; on the one hand subjecting them to sermons about the evils of wealth, and on the other hand expecting them to make the substantial gifts that subsidize the church program. How can money, at one and the same time, be a sought-after necessity of life and yet be a handicap to one's spiritual growth? How can money be evil when no one, not even people of God, can do without it?

Money supported Albert Schweitzer in the steaming jungles of Africa where he labored unselfishly for the natives. Gandhi, in his extreme poverty, going about the land of India with his loin cloth and a little spinning wheel, giving the image of abject poverty, required a lot of money to care for him and his entourage. One of his followers said, "It takes an awful lot of money to keep Gandhi living in poverty." Even Jesus and his disciples were supported by money. This aspect of his ministry is rarely considered, since Jesus has been given the image of a magic-worker who would simply pull money out of the air. In the eighth chapter of Luke, there is a very revealing phrase: "Certain women . . . ministered unto him of their substance" (Lk. 8:2–3 KJV). What could be clearer than that some of his followers were women of means who simply paid much of the expenses.

Jesus clearly accepted his fiscal responsibility. Note how he agreed to pay the Roman head tax that had been levied on his group. He instructed Peter, the fisherman, to go to the sea and catch a fish, in the mouth of which he would find a gold coin. Traditionalists have viewed this as one of the great miracles of the Bible, seemingly abrogating the economic process. This is an excellent example of the need to understand the contemporary use of idiom and metaphor in order to make an accurate translation from one language and culture to another. In clearly identifiable idiomatic language, Jesus was saying to Peter, "Go out and bring in a catch of fish, sell it in the marketplace, and you will have sufficient money to pay the tax." It is a common kind of idiom. Ranchers in the West often say of a steer, "He's worth $40 on the hoof," and in India, it might be said of an ox, "You will find thirty pieces of silver in his horn." Jesus indicated his willingness to work within the system when he commented at this time, "Render therefore unto Caesar the things which are Caesar's; and unto God the things that are God's" (Mt. 22:21 KJV).

One thing is certain: in the world, a monetary means of exchange is indispensable. Without money, there could be no civilization. Culture and currency are intimately related. Barter belongs to primitive and savage peoples. People had to develop a symbol that would bind people together in their commercial relationships with the spiritual ideas of faith and credit before there could evolve a civilized society.

Through the ages, hundreds of different objects have served as the medium of exchange including such things as slaves, salt, gun powder, and the jawbones of pigs. You may have seen pictures of the seven-foot-high pieces of stone money on the South Pacific island of Yap. Wherever any culture has sprung up, you can be sure you will find some form of monetary system.

What is money? The economists have had a problem defining it other than in terms of the function it performs. British economist Sir Ralph Hawtery says, "Money is one of those concepts which, like a teaspoon or an umbrella, but unlike an earthquake or a butter cup, are definable primarily by the use or purpose which they serve." Money is not real wealth at all. Rather it is a device for measuring wealth. Note, for instance, that if the Federal Reserve System should increase the quantity of money in the country by dumping a billion dollars into circulation overnight, it would not add one thing to the country's wealth.

What is money? A piece of paper? Who would stoop down and pick up a dirty piece of paper lying in the gutter? Yet if this dirty piece of paper has the official imprint of the United States government on it along with the figures "100" on its corners, who would not leap upon it and put this dirty paper in his or her pocket as a prized possession?

So then, what is money? Money is an enabling symbol. It is a tangible representation of intangible universal substance, which enables you to provide food, shelter, clothing, entertainment, books, leisure, and security against want. How does it do this? You do not build your house out of paper dollars, and you don't eat the coins. Money is an enabling symbol that gives rise to faith and trust, credit and cooperation, which starts a flow of activity. I take fifty dollars and hand it to the grocer and receive food in exchange. The grocer gives the money to the food distributors, and they to the suppliers, and they to the farmer, who uses the money to buy seed and feed. Round and round it goes in a process that we call the economy. But in back of it all comes the basic substance of life, harnessed and directed by the activity of faith.

Get the positive thought: *Money is good! Money is God in action!* Speak these words over a few times. It is not to make an object of getting money or loving money for itself. We simply want to eliminate some of the negatives with which we have surrounded it. Money is good! You don't have to feel guilty about having it. It is a currency or creative flow of divine activity.

Money passes through your hands many times a day. It may be a little money if you should happen to be on welfare or living on your Social Security, or it may be millions if you are a person of affluence. But you are constantly buying and selling and earning and spending. More than you may be aware of, money is an extension of the person who uses it. Your thoughts and feelings color it, making it "filthy lucre" or blessed divine substance. If you think positively and creatively about your money, you actually multiply its effectiveness. If you criticize and depreciate it, you actually tend to dissipate it and repel it from you.

It seems logical to assume that money always represents abundance, but it doesn't. For most persons, at least much of the time, money is a symbol of lack. We tend to think of it in relationship to what we would like to have or think we should have. For instance, the figure on your paycheck may well symbolize to you injustice ("they don't pay me enough"), unappreciation ("they are not aware of how valuable I am to the company"), and insufficiency ("how can I live on this salary with all the rising costs?").

If you were asked, "How much do you earn a week?" probably your reply would be, "I only make $200 (or $500 or $1000) a week." But why the only? It is a self-inventory term that is commonly used, but it invariably represents limitation. How much money do you have on your person? "Only $43.32!" Again, why the only? As long as this "onlyness" consciousness is in any way identified with your money, you are depreciating it.

Take stock of all your references to money. It is often said about some financial commitment, "Oh, it's only money!" It is a subtle put-down. It is just such flippant attitudes toward money that create a resistance which blocks the flow of the substance current. (Note that "current" gives rise to the word *currency*.) Have you ever noticed the grim expressions on people's faces as they go to their purses or wallets for money to make a payment? It would strongly suggest a negative identification. The need is to turn this around. Money is good! Money is God in action! Feel good about making contact with the divine current. Handle the currency with the joyous feeling that you are in the flow.

Take out a dollar bill and hold it in your hands. Turn it face up (the side with the black printing). The identifying feature of the dollar on this side is the number "1" (or "5" or "10" and so on). The number represents the bill's limitation. It is one dollar, not one penny more. Now turn the bill over to the green side. Focus your attention on that lovely inscription, "IN GOD WE TRUST." Note what you have done. As you turned the bill over, you turned from limitation to limitlessness, from "onlyness" (it is only one dollar) to Allness (I put my trust in the Allness of infinite supply).

Remember, your money is an extension of you. It is a symbol of limitation or of limitlessness according to how you think while you use it. When you receive or spend money, "think green," and as you handle it, "keep the green side up" (speaking figuratively, of course). In other words, keep your identity with money as a symbol of limitless God-substance. I buy an item at the newsstand, and I hand the man one dollar ("Render . . . unto Caesar the things which are Caesar's"), but as I do this, I am conscious that I am giving way to the limitless flow of prospering substance (". . . unto God the things that are God's"). It is a mental discipline that can help immeasurably in building and maintaining a prosperity consciousness.

H. C. Mattern had failed in nearly everything he had done. His marriage was broken, his business had failed, and he was down to his very last dollar. He became so desperate that he attempted suicide, but he failed at that too. Then he was struck by the "Promethean urge," which is the upward pull of Spirit in man. Life is always biased on the side of healing and renewal. If you are patient and open, the light breaks through the dark clouds and comes rushing into your hungry heart. So, something happened to Mattern. In an amazing turnabout, he stopped looking to externals for help. He no longer looked at money as a goal or as a measuring stick of success. He began seeing money as a current of the divine resource. And the one dollar he had was an adequate reminder of that resource. After all, it was the reminder he needed, not Fort Knox. He turned the green side up: "In God I trust—really!"

Ultimately, into his awareness came an idea that gave rise to a creative business enterprise that made him a great amount of money—enough to have made him a wealthy man had he saved his money. Instead, he gave most of it away as it came. He said, "Since I stopped looking to money I have been happy and prosperous. Why go back to the old way now?"

The first thing Mattern had to overcome was the feeling of needing money. Have you had a time of financial stringency and cried out, "I need money"? It is a confusion of priorities. More importantly, you need faith. You need a flow of creativity. You need ideas. Actually, it could be said that your money needs you. As long as you have impressed on your money the thought of insufficiency, it will continue to misrepresent you in your time of need. But if you consciously imbue your money with the idea of abundance, it will begin to work for you in a positive way. Suddenly the seemingly little supply becomes dynamic seed money, giving rise to unbelievable increase.

The falls at Niagara would be of no use to us without the power plants that line the banks to convert the raw energy into usable electric current that blesses thousands of homes with power. In the same way, your money needs your creative ideas to become of use to you. It needs your faith and your vision. You see, you always have this vital choice. You may not have nearly enough money to meet the need, but you always have within you *the inlet that may become the outlet to all there is in God*. As you "turn the green side up" and become centered in the divine flow, you create the condition in consciousness that makes the result inevitable. You are never further than one idea away from all the wealth in the Universe.

Prosperity books use as examples tycoons such as Henry Ford and Andrew Carnegie to illustrate how you, too, can become a millionaire. The fact is, these people did not set out to make money at all. In each case, there was the sudden or progressive unfoldment of an idea, which in turn was translated into automobile plants and steel mills. The real substance that made it all possible was ideas. Ideas are the flowing forth into mind of the wealth of the Universe. And every person has his or her own unique pipeline to the Allness of Infinite Mind. Thus if you want to pattern your life after some tycoon role model, call to mind Paul's great thought and let the same Mind that was in Christ Jesus be in you. You have open access in you to the same Infinite Mind resource as that which flowed so creatively through any person who has amassed great wealth by producing great things.

Another interesting facet of the money enigma: the paper money you have in your pocket or purse at one time represented so much gold or silver. Now there are many times as much currency as hard metal to back it up. Economists cringe and politicians view with alarm at what some consider the basic cause of inflation. Perhaps it is! But for you, it is important to remember that wealth is not in money . . . wealth is in ideas. And ideas can be controlled through the discipline of mind.

As an example, suppose that all numbers are made out of little metal pieces and that it is against the law to print numbers for yourself. Every time you need to do a sum in arithmetic, you have to provide yourself with a supply of numbers, arrange them in proper order, and then work out your problem with them. And if the problem is extremely complicated, such as working on your income tax returns, you might have to go to a numbers bank to get a greater supply. Sound ridiculous? Of course numbers are not things. They are only ideas, and you can add or subtract or multiply or divide them as often as you like. You can have all the numbers you can use. And you can work out problems in your head without even writing them on paper, for they, too, are enabling symbols.

Note the parallel with money. Money is an enabling symbol, but it symbolizes something that is limitless. If you are experiencing lack, you may go to a friend or to the bank to get a supply of those things we call dollars. It is interesting to note that Jesus went forth *without scrip or purse*. In other words, he could work the figures in his head. This refers to the rich mentality that attracts substance. As one man said, "Since I became aware that I am an individualized expression of the infinite flow of substance, I feel prosperous at all times. And the most amazing thing is the way money flows to me from all directions. I simply can't keep it away from me."

In the business world, there is a common delusion that material capital, usually referred to as "principal," is almighty. In other words, money is all-important, nothing else matters. This is completely erroneous. Any successful business venture demonstrates that integrity and service have been the keys to the public confidence which created the success. J. Pierpont Morgan is reputed to have said, when he was asked about his practice of making large business loans on slender credit, "I look at his character before I look at his collateral." In other words, he was more concerned with what the person was worthy of than what he was worth. In every case, the real capital was spiritual principle.

The key to any condition of lack is spiritual principle.

Poverty is not corrected by dollars but by nonmaterial substance. You can give the man begging for money a dollar (or five or ten) to buy a cup of coffee, but even if he does buy the coffee and something to eat, before the day is out he will be hungry again. Unless there is a change in his consciousness, unless he awakens to the Truth about his own relationship with the Universe and gets in tune with his own unique flow of supply from within, nothing has really changed. Poverty programs must begin to think "hand-up" instead of "handout." The poverty of any society can be controlled, but only as people are introduced to the idea expressed by Emerson that every person "is an inlet and may become an outlet to all there is in God."

The prospering element will always be nonmaterial substance. And there can never be a shortage of this substance in the Universe. Even within an apparent condition of indigence, the only lack in terms of the principle is the thought of lack. You are always as rich as you think you are and the only poverty is of the mind. So you can begin to do something about your financial position in life by reshaping your attitudes about yourself, about money in general, and about your work or investments as the source of your money in particular.

Remember: Money is good! Money is God in action! Money is directly or indirectly involved in everything we do all day long. So it is imperative that we have a positive attitude about it. Appreciate it, bless it, keep open to its flow.

Charles Fillmore gives some important thoughts about handling money positively and creatively:

Watch your thoughts when you are handling your money, because your money is attached through your mind to the one source of all substance and all money. When you think of your money, which is visible, as something directly attached to an invisible source that is giving or withholding according to your thought, you have the key to all riches and all lack.

Never allow money of any kind or amount to pass through your hands without blessing it, whether it is coming to you or going from you. To "bless" is an old-fashioned practice that needs to be rediscovered. The word means "to confer prosperity or happiness upon." In other words, in handling money on any occasion, be sure to give it the imprint of positive attitudes. The money is a wonderful symbol of God's substance. Give thanks that it is continually pointing you toward the limitlessness of universal supply. Keep the awareness that it is currency, a movement of the divine flow. When it comes to you, give thanks that it has flowed from the Infinite through your job or investment. When it goes from you, give thanks that there is no depletion, but actually an increase because you have kept it flowing.

It is interesting what we do with symbols. Consider the Christian Cross. Originally, the Cross had a very dynamic meaning. It was the symbol of overcoming, of victory, pointing ahead to the empty tomb and the great demonstration of the resurrection principle. But as the years passed, it became a symbol of tragedy and pain and humiliation. The simple Cross was adorned with the figure of Jesus dying an agonizing death. There is an oriental adage that says, "The teacher points to the Truth; the student worships the pointer." Thus the Cross has become an object of worship. This is precisely what all too often happens with money. Money is a symbol of the currency or flow of universal substance. And how we tend to worship the pointer! Money becomes the object of life's search for meaning.

Thus whenever you experience any evidence of the flow of substance in your paycheck, through investments, or as you pay your bills or buy something at the supermarket, bless it. Keep the green side up. Let it suggest to you, "In God I trust—really!" Determine that your money will always be a symbol of abundance, not of limitation. When you are firmly established in a balance of spiritual well-being, there will be a right and natural movement in your affairs wherein substance will flow forth freely in terms of the money to enable you to experience life more abundant.

CHAPTER 10

Discover the Wonder of Giving

In a book devoted to the theme of prosperity, it might be assumed that the emphasis would be on "how to get." Perhaps by now you will understand why we say that such an emphasis is not only grossly materialistic, but it is also extremely misleading. Any study of prosperity fails unless it teaches you how (and why) to give. And that is precisely what this chapter is about.

Giving does not refer simply to money. It is a process that may involve money, but it also involves your work and the many ways in which you make contact with life. Giving is basically an attitude with which you touch things.

The word *giving* has become so completely identified with pious acts of philanthropy that it is difficult to think of the word without referring to the "commercial of the church." The emphasis has been on what the gift is to and what rewards come back in the form of "heavenly grace," a name on the stained-glass window and a healthy deduction on the income tax return.

In the past forty years there has been a dramatic upheaval in the lifestyles of people of the Western world, brought about by the influence of a number of well-publicized revolutions. The womens' movement has brought about notable gains in terms of freedoms at home and at work. Computers have invaded and changed our whole lives. Sexual attitudes have become startlingly relaxed. Minority groups have moved up into the middle class in increasing numbers. But there is another revolution that has had widespread impact. It is the predominant attitude toward money and success and the acceptable methods of achievement. Gradually there has evolved an emphasis on getting what you want when you want it at any cost. As we've said, some of the most widely read books in recent years have dealt with themes such as assertiveness, intimidation, positive selfishness, and it's okay to be greedy. One writer talks about the "new wave of Machiavellianism." In this, any means, no matter how unscrupulous, is justified in working for achievement. Getting there is all that counts, whether or not the person earns the right to be there.

Ideas like this have come to popularity among people who are lost and confused in the world of materiality, people who have asked the question, "What is life?" and have come up empty. Thus they have concluded that life is a competition among people who have no alternative other than to push aggressively out into the world and strive relentlessly to get the most for the least.

However, this misses the very important point that life is not lived from outside-in, but from inside-out. Unless we understand this, we miss the whole meaning of life. The purpose of life is not acquisition but unfoldment and personal development. Even in the teaching of metaphysics, there has been a tremendous swing toward this revolutionary attitude toward money and things. Thus many books and courses by teachers of Truth emphasize "how-to" techniques for demonstrating money and possessions and jobs and success. The constant theme is get, get, get, get. Just hold the right thought, and you can get anything you want. And the grossest level of materialism is reached when Truth groups are led in singing prosperity songs in which the refrain affirms, "Money, money, money!" A sad derogation of a beautiful, spiritual process.

This contemporary trend toward materialism is attributable in a large part to the sad neglect of the church in teaching the law of giving. Religious institutions have failed miserably in this respect, undoubtedly because they have been preoccupied with their own need to receive support. Preachers have talked of giving as "returning to God a portion of one's income." Churchgoers have been lulled into a pious acceptance of this form of idealism.

However, it completely skirts the issue of inward-rooted giving as it deals with an anemic God of the skies who bargains with us for a giving return.

Jesus said, "Consider the lilies of the field, how they grow" (Mt. 6:28). By nature's law, the lily grows and unfolds from a bulb to a flower. It is a discernable unfoldment from within outward. There is no obligation for the flower to return a portion of its fragrance and color and form to nature. There is no way it could do this even if it wanted to do so, because life is a forward, growing, unfolding experience. Don't miss the implication of this homely illustration. Your life is God's gift to you. What you do with it is your gift to God.

Two men were engaged in an animated conversation. As the discussion grew increasingly heated, one of the men was heard to say, "Just tell me one thing, what's in it for me?" It is an attitude that is all too common. What's in it for me? Not, how can I give more to the job or relationship, but how can I be sure that I get mine?

An article on the editorial page of the *New York Times* recently discussed the lack of any sense of the "old-fashioned work ethic" among the new generation of people ages twenty to thirty moving into the job market. A personnel manager is quoted as referring to the new "benefit bums." He says that during an interview these people hardly listen to the duties of the job being explained. They ask questions about salary, vacations, sick days, and other benefits and "perks." They shop employers for benefits. That to them seems to be the essence of employment. They are ready to take but not to give. Once hired, the syndrome continues. They are chronically late in the morning; they take the longest coffee breaks and lunch hours; and they spend large segments of the day in time-consuming conversations. And then they get ready for the 5 o'clock quitting time at 4:30. The personnel manager says that their skills are low and their motivation even lower. Further, they seem to suffer from strange maladies, such as "Monday affliction," and "Friday afternoon paralysis." They may be products of the spreading "welfare psychosis" that has afflicted countless families in the past generation. They seem to say to the employer, "Pay me because I am here, not for what I can do."

If true, this is a stirring indictment of the contemporary generation. Perhaps it is overstated, more of a caricature of the actual situation. However, anyone who has worked with people in the supervisory capacity will readily agree that there are two general types of people in life: *the givers and the takers.* A word of caution: please don't agree with this judgmentally—thinking, "Oh, yes, I know many people who are takers." We are not dealing with "they" or "them." We are dealing with you. See it as a test for yourself. We are not trying to change others. Our goal in this book is to help *you* to be "transformed by the renewal of your mind" (Rom. 12:2).

The *takers* are the people who believe that their lives will always be the total of what they can get from the world. They are always thinking get, get, get. They plan and scheme ways to get what they want in money, in love, in happiness, and in all kinds of good. No matter that they may be applying metaphysical techniques, they still may very well be takers. But whatever may be their spiritual ideals or lack of any, no matter what they take, they can never know peace or security or fulfillment.

The *givers*, on the other hand, are convinced that life is a giving process. Thus their subtle motivation in all their ways is to give themselves away, in love, in service, and in all the many helpful ways they can invest themselves. They are always secure, for they intuitively know that their good flows from within.

In the third chapter of John, sixteenth verse, is the classic statement so often repeated by Christian fundamentalists: "For God so loved the world, that he gave his only begotten Son, that whosoever believeth in him should not perish, but have everlasting life" (KJV). It is commonly thought and taught that this refers to Jesus, that Jesus is the only begotten Son, and by believing in him, we attain eternal life. The whole structure of the traditional Christian view rests on this foundation concept, which is by and large a misconception. Meister Eckehart, a medieval mystic monk, gives the key that unlocks the true meaning of John 3:16: "God never begot but one son, but the eternal is forever begetting the only-begotten." In other words, God so loved you that God gave you that which is begotten only of God. While much of your human self bears the influence of your parental background and also of your sociological experiences in life, yet there is that of you, the whole person of you, the Self of you, which is begotten only of God. And if you believe in what Paul calls the Christ in you, you begin to experience life on an eternal vibration. What a transcendent idea, that you have your own unique flow of the divine! This is why Emerson talks of the need for each person to have his or her own "first-hand and immediate experience of God."

However, the most important aspect of John 3:16 is "for God so loved the world that he gave." God is the divine givingness of the Universe. And you are created in the image-likeness of this divine givingness. You cannot make any sense out of life or realize the free flow of substance in your experience until you begin to see yourself as a giver. It may mean a complete turnaround in your approach to life, where you think "give" instead of "get." In your spiritual quest, you are seeking to establish yourself in a unitive relationship with the divine flow. You can never really achieve this level of consciousness until giving becomes the main thrust of your life. And when it does, when you discover the wonder of giving, you become, unblushingly, an incurable giver. Meditate long on this point, for it is one of the most important keys of the prosperity law.

Life for the whole person is a giving process. We are not talking specifically about church giving, giving to charity, and so forth. There are many channels through which your giving may be funneled. We are talking about attitudes toward life, the basic awareness that life is a matter of developing or unfolding from within. It is knowing that life is not something to get but something to express. It is the fulfilling awareness that your business is always the express business, no matter what name your worldly vocation may bear.

There is an inspired painting by a German artist, Rosenthal, entitled *The Blessing of Work*. It depicts a young boy carving a life-size picture of the Virgin Mary. The almost-completed figure towers above the young artist, and while he works intently carving the details of the feet, Mary looks down upon him with love and with outstretched arms, blessing him. While he is giving himself in the creative flow, he is dynamically receiving immeasurably in return. The painting reveals much more: light is streaming through the open window, its rays bathing him with an aura of illumination. On a large plaque on the wall, a heavenly choir is singing paeons of praise directly toward him. By his side, there is what we assume to be a picture of his mother which he is using for a model, and with hands clasped in devotion, she is blessing him. Thus the whole tone of the work suggests that the whole Universe is rushing, streaming, pouring into the boy, while he quietly gives himself in creative effort. It is a beautiful visual testimony to Jesus: "Give and you shall receive."

It could be cynically asked, What's in it for the boy? The sculptured figure may one day bring him fame and fortune. Or it could wind up in an attic somewhere, discarded and useless. But the important thing is, nothing can ever exceed or detract from the compensation that the boy is receiving at the instant while he is working. Even more, that sculptured piece could never be duplicated by one who lacks his giving attitude, which is an important facet of his genius. There are many skilled, even exceptional, painters, sculptors, composers, and builders. But the real genius is the one whose skill is held up, like an aeolian harp, through which the winds of selfless giving blow steadily, creating ethereal music. Someone has said that architecture is "frozen music." Perhaps it is true of all great art. Such is the law of giving.

"What's in it for me?" You may be saying this of your present job, perhaps out of a feeling that you are not adequately compensated for the work you do and the responsibilities you shoulder. If you discover the wonder of giving, you will find a great blessing of inner fulfillment in your work, which will lead to better work, and by the law of causation, to a greater experience of affluence, which may come through your job or through many different channels. The law is exact: If you *give*, really work in a giving consciousness, you *must* receive. If you, at this point, still ask the question, "What's in it for me?" then you are being grossly underpaid, even if your salary is in six figures. If all you get out of your work is a paycheck, you are short-changing yourself.

An itinerant preacher went to a neighboring parish to

preach by invitation, taking his young son with him. As they entered the church, he saw a contribution box, and following his good instincts, he deposited a half-dollar. After his sermon was completed and the congregation had departed, the minister-host said, "We are not a very prosperous parish, and all we can pay is what is in the contribution box." So he opened the box and presented the visitor with the half-dollar, all that had been put in. The visitor thanked him and went his way, if not rejoicing, at least resigned. They walked in silence for a distance, and then the wise young lad said, "Gee, Dad, if you had put more in you would have gotten more out." Such is the great law of giving.

Who has not exclaimed at some low moment of his life, "My life has no meaning"? This sense of meaninglessness is the greatest cause of depression and even of compulsive addiction in the form of overeating, alcoholism, and drug addiction. But you see, life doesn't have meaning. Only you have meaning. It makes about as much sense to say, "My life has no meaning," as it does to stand in a dark cave with an unlit flashlight in your hand and say, "This place has no light." Jesus would say, "Let your light shine." Meaning is not to be found "out there," in a job, in a person, or in a relationship. Meaning is something you release from within yourself. You put meaning into your work, into your experiences, and into every relationship with people. Many persons find great meaning in their lives through a kind of work that would be a drag to someone else. It is not the work but the sense of giving in which it is done.

When a young person begins thinking about career opportunities, she may ask, "What is a good field to get into?" It is a critical moment in her life. If she asks you out of respect for your experience and maturity, you are in a position to get to her with an insight that can be a blessing to her all through her life. She is standing at the crossroads, with one road ahead leading in the way of getting and the other leading in the way of giving. If you are wise, you will answer her question by asking her another question, "Do you mean what is a good field or what is a good field for you?" She may then ask, "But what field will pay the most money?" You should wisely respond: "That is a question you should resist as long as you can. In the long run, the work that will prosper is the work you can put yourself into with the most enthusiasm. If you take that which offers the greatest immediate return, you may well frustrate your own potential, even your eventual earning power." She may persist, "But shouldn't I try to find a job with a future?" You can then say: "There is no future in any job. The future is in you. When you find your right place, you will release that which will make for a good and happy and successful future."

The president of a great railroad was on an inspection tour when he encountered a laborer in a section gang with whom he had worked in that same work some forty years earlier. He greeted his old friend warmly, remembering the "old days." The tired old laborer said, "Bert, you've gone a long way from the time when we were laying tracks together." The executive said, "No, Sam, that isn't quite correct. You were laying tracks; I was building a railroad." Therein lies the difference. If you are a secretary, do you just type letters or are you helping your company sell products? If you work in a sanitation department, do you simply sweep streets or are you helping to maintain the health of the community?

Analyze your attitude toward your work. Do you go to work with a sense of eagerness in the morning? Is your work a happy experience? If not, you are probably tired toward the latter part of the day and exhausted when you arrive home in the evening. You may attribute the exhaustion to the amount of work you do. But it is more likely the result of your resistance and resentment. You may feel unappreciated, underpaid, overworked. And it could be true. But your life is lived from within out. No matter what conditions prevail in your place of work, what happens in you is the result of your consciousness. You might find a co-worker in your department who is perfectly happy there. The difference is not that he or she is treated differently but that he or she treats the work to be done differently. Begin thinking *give,* and the resistance and the fatigue that it spawns will quickly leave.

One of the most significant phrases in the Bible is "wait on the Lord" (several references in Proverbs and Psalms). It comes from the Hebrew word *qavah*, which means "to bind together." Thus to wait on the Lord does not mean to sit down and fold your hands in the faith that God will do it all for you. The fact is, God can do no more for you than God can do through you. It is not inaction or procrastination. "Wait on the Lord" means to get yourself integrated in consciousness with the divine flow. It is so very important, before undertaking any project, to wait on the Lord in a conscious prayer experience in which you turn your thoughts inward and establish yourself in the flow of the creative process. It is an important moment, "God's moment," before you go to work or before you set out to find a job. Just become very still and centered, sense the creative energy of Spirit tingling in your fingertips, guiding your hands, directing your footsteps, putting words into your mouth, helping you to do the things that need to be done, to do them easily and to do them well.

The first thing that will happen is that you will forget that there is a reward dangling before you for the work you do. You will no longer be working for money. You will be paid, of course, but it will be an added compensation for doing the thing you love to do. You will have a strong urge to do all that you can to the utmost of your skill. There isn't a job in all the world that can't be done better than it is being done when workers change their attitude about it. And, no one is doing right by themselves or their employer if they simply rock along, going through the motions of doing their work. If you want to work for the kind of consciousness that will maintain you in the giving flow, begin every day with the commitment:

I will do what I do better and better and better, and I will do more and more of what I do.

When you begin to understand this life principle, you will know that there is a wellspring of life, substance, and intelligence within you, and that yours is the privilege at any time of giving way to its flow. This may lead to one of the most important realizations that will ever come to you: if ever there is a lack of any kind, whether it is a need for employment or for money or for guidance or even for healing, *something is blocking the flow.* And the most effective remedy: Give! You may be thinking, But I need to receive. My hands are empty. I need someone to give to me. But you see, under the law of giving, when things get tight, something's got to give. Look for some way to start the giving flow. Make a commitment to some kind of giving. Not a bargain with God, for that is a kind of pious procrastination. ("Okay, God, if You do so and so, then I will do so and so. But You do it first.") Rather, make a covenant with yourself. It could be an offering of thanks to a place from which you have been receiving spiritual help; it could be greater giving in your work; it could be doing something for another person who is in need; it could even be simply giving away some seldom-used possession.

Something's got to give! It is so easy to get down in consciousness from the desperate need to receive. You might even think, When I demonstrate the supply, I will send a gift to the church. Why not give now? And if there is no money, go down to the church or some other non-profit organization and volunteer your services. If you are unemployed, get into the giving flow by giving your services to some community activity or offer to help some young person who may be struggling in a new business enterprise or just stay home and keep your hands and mind involved in creative activity. Take some time to go through your attic and closets and drawers to find all the seldom-used or never-used possessions that can bless someone richly and derive a great thrill and spiritual fulfillment by giving. There is never a time when you can't find some way to start the giving flow, which in turn will open the way to the receiving of your good.

Jesus clearly articulated the divine law: "Give, and it will be given to you" (Lk. 6:38). The divine flow requires but one thing of you: your consent to be a receiving channel. It is like the water faucet which must be opened to the flow in order that the water may pour forth freely. Jesus was stressing the need to get into a giving consciousness in order to sustain the flow of good into your life. He did not mean simply money giving. Often the religious book or teacher will talk out of a self-interest and insist that the giving must go to the church. The giving is a state of consciousness that may eventuate in many different ways. But the important thing is to think, give! Say to yourself, "I will think give today. I will think give every day of my life." The law is clear. It promises: Think give, and you will get. It is a fundamental key to achieving prosperity.

A truly giving consciousness is the creative alternative to the worldly emphasis on winning through intimidation or succeeding through positive selfishness. It is the better way. And a committed giver is an incurably happy person, a secure person, a satisfied person, and a prosperous person.

When you discover the wonder of giving, you will wonder how you could have lived so long in any other way. It is the key that makes Truth work, that opens the door to the good you have been seeking, and that gives life that added glow. It can be one of the great discoveries of your life. When you become a committed giver, you can no more go back to the old way of living than you can go back to life in prehistoric times.

There is a new world awaiting you, a new level of life that can open to you, and a new experience of the dynamism of Truth which you have been studying. Discover the wonder of giving. It is the better way. And the day will come when you will insist that it is the *only* way.

A New Look at Tithing

A study of the subject of prosperity invariably includes the practice of tithing. In most cases, it is taught with a dogmatism that is unparalleled in the whole study of Truth. Tithers swear by the practice and speak glowingly of the benefits that have come to them. However, many persons, feeling the "pinch" of economic stringency, have great reservations about it.

The tithing idea is often given mystical roots, dating biblically to the book of Genesis, where Abraham gave a tithe of all he had to Melchizedek, king of Salem, who had blessed him. Today there are whole religious denominations that require tithing of all their adherents. Many other religious groups suggest it as a helpful discipline. Building on the foundation belief that tithing is God's law, many highly persuasive arguments are set forth.

At the very outset, let us establish the point that tithing is an excellent practice that we strongly recommend to anyone who is seeking to change his or her life from indigence to affluence. And in this chapter, we want to probe deeply into the practice, beyond the superficial, illogical, and materialistic way it is normally approached. Tithing is normally encouraged for all the wrong reasons. Some of the claims made and the arguments set forth make the tithing concept a gross materialization of a beautiful, spiritual law.

Is the practice of tithing a fundamental in this "new insight in Truth"? Is it biblical? Was it a part of Jesus' teaching? Where are the origins? And how has it evolved to contemporary times?

Bible students know that the Old Testament often refers to the practice of tithing. The classic reference is Malachi 3:10 (ASV): "Bring ye the whole tithe into the storehouse, that there may be food in my house, and prove me now herewith, saith Jehovah of hosts, if I will not open you the windows of heaven, and pour you out a blessing, that there shall not be room enough to receive it." It is a beautiful statement, sheer poetry! Who could take issue with it? Of course there is no reason to do so. However, neither is there reason to not examine the practice in the time of Malachi.

Under Levitical law, the tithe was a form of taxation required of the Hebrews, a portion of the produce of the earth and of their herds. It wasn't a love offering or charitable contribution at all. In a religious form of government, a theocracy, tithing has often been the method of creating revenues to support the government. Since God is the true ruler, it is easily rationalized that the government treasury is the storehouse of the Lord.

In early Israel, under the leadership of Moses, the new nation was formed by dividing the body into twelve tribes. One of the tribes, the tribe of Levi, was singled out to serve as the priestly class. Again, in a theocracy, the government is managed by the priests. Thus the Levites became the bureaucracy, and the system by which they were supported was the tithe. There was nothing voluntary about it. The Mosaic code was rigidly enforced, and in some cases, infractions were punishable by death. This is the biblical source from which our contemporary practice of tithing has derived.

However, the tithe did not originate there. Some form of tithing was practiced almost universally throughout all the ancient world. We find evidences of it in Babylonia, in Persia, in Egypt, in Rome, and even in China. Keep in mind that it was a tithe tax, which probably originated as a tribute laid down by a shrewd conqueror or ruler on his subjects. It may be assumed that the custom of dedicating a tenth of the spoils of war "to the gods" in time gave rise to a religious extension of the phrase ("giving the tenth to God"). It is highly likely that when Abraham gave a tithe of his flocks to Melchizedek, the king of Salem, he was actually paying a tribute to the ruler for safe passage through his land.

Not understanding all this, or possibly not wanting to see it, religious teachers and writers, wanting to cite authorities for the contemporary tithing practice, have pointed to all the many instances in the Old Testament where tithe is referred to. The argument that is usually used is "if a tenth was required under law in those olden times, it is certainly no less fitting that we should give it cheerfully now." Now, without judging the merits of tithing, isn't this line of reasoning somewhat illogical? Under their law, the Israelites were bound to many restrictive observances. There are references to people actually being stoned to death for nothing more than gathering wheat on the Sabbath day, for this was a clear infraction of the fourth commandment. But we do not put people to death in modern times for playing golf on Sunday. Ah, but times have changed, we say. But why should the rigidity of the tithing observance remain unchanged, even if it was a giving process in biblical times, which it was not?

Jesus seemed to make a career out of upgrading the laws and observances of the Old Testament into the light and needs of contemporary times. For instance, with many of the commandments, he said in essence, "You have heard it said of old, but I say unto you . . ." Then he gave a practical insight for living. He was no rebel intent on breaking down the rule of ecclesiastical law. He was a Jew, reared in the traditions of the synagogue. And he said, "I have come not to abolish them [the laws] but to fulfill them" (Mt. 5:17).

If you are interested, carefully examine the Ten Commandments. They would appear to be a series of restrictive laws, outlining lines of conduct by which the Israelites must live. However, wise students of practical religion will break them down to their underlying essence, where they can see them as a supportive framework for the spiritually immature. Infants may need playpens and children may need fences to keep them from straying into danger. But as people mature, there must come a time when they *put away childish things.* For instance, a sign of maturity in teenagers is when they decide to come home at a "reasonable" hour because they need the rest for school the following day, not just because their parents say so and will take away their allowance if they disobey. So it is with the idea of tithing. If we can accept the early practice as a form of "mandatory contribution," then, as with the Commandments, it was intended as a trellis by which we might be strengthened in our early period of spiritual growth. But the time must come when we let go of the rigid obligation so that we can spontaneously give in love and freedom and have the satisfaction that our giving equals or even exceeds the tithe.

The discipline of tithing has been strongly stressed by many teachers in the field of New Thought or metaphysics. In view of his constant attempt to upgrade the Mosaic laws and of his clear outline of the principles of abundant living, it might be assumed that Jesus would have much to say on the subject. Actually, Jesus is never quoted in support of tithing. The reason is obvious: he makes only two references to the practice, and in both instances, tithing is referred to as a practice of someone who is being criticized.

In one of his tirades against the Pharisees, Jesus said: "Woe to you, scribes and Pharisees, hypocrites! for you tithe mint and dill and cummin, and have neglected the weightier matters of the law . . . . You blind guides, straining out a gnat and swallowing a camel!" (Mt. 23:23–24) This is certainly not a recommendation of tithing.

In his parable of the Pharisee and the tax collector, the Pharisee stood and prayed "'God, I thank thee that I am not like other men, extortioners, unjust, adulterers, or even like this tax collector. I fast twice a week, I give tithes of all that I get'" (Lk. 18:11–12). Then Jesus said that the tax collector would be justified, not the Pharisee. Again, no tribute to the tithing practice.

This is not to infer that Jesus condemned the practice of tithing. But it is to realize that he saw the keeping of the rigid code of tithing as a ritual far less important than the "weightier matters" of consciousness. And since he did make reference to the subject, certainly if he had felt that tithing was a "must" in his high way of spiritual unfoldment, he would have stated a clear position. But he didn't do so.

It is important to note that Jesus was very specific in his teaching of the law of giving (note that we are drawing a definite distinction between the practice of tithing and the spontaneous process of giving): "Give, and it shall be given unto you; good measure, pressed down, and shaken together, and running over, shall men give into your bosom. For with the same measure that ye mete withal it shall be measured to you again" (Lk. 6:38 KJV).

The Old Testament dealt with the law of giving, which is fundamentally *supportive*, on the basis of the practice of tithing, which was completely *coercive*. Tithing was something the Israelites were required to do. Jesus taught the law of consciousness, that one always has a choice, though one must live with the effects of his or her choice. You receive as you give, and if you would receive more, you can give more. But you have complete freedom.

In Old Testament times, tithing was an enforced discipline laid down for people who did not have the spiritual development to work with divine law. It took its place alongside hundreds of laws and observances governing everything from sanitation to meditation. As training wheels on a bicycle help a youngster to learn to ride unaided, so all these laws were right and appropriate for the people of that day.

This is not to say that we may not be benefited by "training wheels" in many aspects of our sociological and spiritual development. Certainly the practice of tithing is an excellent training process. One may read dozens of testimonials of persons who have gotten themselves on the road to a giving consciousness and who have demonstrated success and prosperity through the disciplined practice of tithing.

One classic example: William Colgate. Before leaving his home in Baltimore to seek his fortune in New York, he was advised by a family friend, an old riverboat captain, "Son, whatever work you do, do it well, take the Lord into partnership, give Him a tenth of all you make, and you will never fail." Soon Colgate was the manager of a Manhattan soap firm, and a few years later he had his own business. He always set aside ten cents of each dollar for charity. On his books, his donations were labeled, "Account with the Lord." As his profits soared, he instructed the bookkeeper to increase the amount to 20 percent, and later to 30 percent.

Ultimately, he was giving 50 percent, and yet the more he gave, the more his business flourished. Among many philanthropic gestures that his tithes gave life to were the American Bible Society, of which he was one of the first directors, and Colgate University, which now bears his name. It is a classic story of American enterprise based on the prospering influence of tithing.

It is unfortunate, however, and also misleading, that tithing is presented as a divine law rather than as a training discipline by which to work toward knowledge of the law of giving. Sometimes it is said that tithing is a magic cure for all ills. But there is no magic whatever in tithing. If prosperity or healing results from tithing, it has come through the fulfilling of the law: As you give, so you receive. Bicycle riding is based on the law of balance working with the law of inertia. The training wheels have nothing to do with the laws by which the bicycle is propelled. They simply help the rider to experience the working of the law.

Why do we insist on this distinction? Tithing is not an end but a helpful means toward the end of living totally in a giving consciousness. Too often institutions "sell" the tithing practice as a way of achieving sustained support. Now, an effective religious organization is certainly worthy of support. But fundamental to this effectiveness is helping people to understand the full scope of the law of giving. Totally overlooked is the teaching responsibility to lead the person to an understanding of the process of *giving way* to the divine flow. Little wonder that some people refer to tithing as the "commercial of the church," a tragic derogation of a beautiful idea.

Books on the subject of tithing are often adorned with dollar signs, suggesting that tithing is an infallible way to get rich. Again, a sickening materialization of a beautiful

Truth. To tithe as a kind of good investment, expecting to get back more than one gives, is not truly giving. It is a kind of bartering, a selfish attempt to work the law instead of letting the law work you.

This materialistic approach to tithing is widespread, and ours may well be a voice crying in the wilderness. We ask only that the tither, or the person weighing the merits of the practice, think the matter through carefully.

If people get into the tithe-your-way-to-riches-and-success consciousness, they are building their house on sand. With dollar signs in their eyes, they are more concerned with what they are giving *to* than what they are giving *from*. This need not be the case. It is a question of motivation. One needs to face up to some hard questions: Do I tithe to get things or to get a greater awareness of divine law? Do I analyze the effectiveness of my tithing on the basis of my income or my general well-being?

Let us not be misunderstood on this point: giving is a fundamental spiritual law. You cannot live without giving, as you cannot live without breathing. You inhale and you exhale, on and on constantly. It is a part of the vital process of life. But there is no rule that says you must inhale so many cubic inches of air. It depends on your lung capacity and on the requirements in terms of your level of exertion. Now, it may be that a person is not breathing correctly, so a specialist may give the person some breathing exercises which can be helpful in restoring balance. In the same sense, tithing can be an excellent program to help you become established in the giving-receiving rhythm.

The principle is, as we stressed in the previous chapter, in any complications you may experience in life, the most effective road to overcoming is through giving. However, tithing is not necessarily the way to a giving consciousness. It is possible that you may neglect the consciousness of giving while you are enthralled with the "magic" of tithing. Here is an example: A person desires success and prosperity in her work. She is convinced that tithing will work its magic for her. After several months of tithing, when nothing shows signs of changing in her office, she begins to get discouraged. She feels that through tithing she has "paid her dues" so a promotion or raise in salary should come through. Yet if you analyze her job performance as her superiors do, you will immediately see that she does not give much of herself to her work, is not very effective, frequently arrives late, and talks to co-workers incessantly during the day. She feels that, by tithing, things will change for her. It could be said there is a raise in salary for her which will become effective when she does. She tithes but she does not give. She needs to begin to think *give*, to become service-oriented, to go the extra mile, to be more creative in her work. Tithing can be a way of getting into a giving consciousness, but it is not a substitute for a giving attitude.

The great need is to give way to the divine flow, and tithing can be an excellent means of achieving the giving

consciousness. However, the giving must involve something more than the writing of a tithe check. Malachi
refers to the *whole tithe*. This means all of us and not just
all of our money. When Jesus criticized the Pharisees for
tithing without love, he could have been implying that
they tithed decimally and not spiritually.

The *whole tithe* would appear to be exemplified in the
incident where Peter and John were accosted by a crippled
beggar at the Temple. Peter said to the man, "I have no silver and gold, but I give you what I have; in the name of
Jesus Christ of Nazareth, walk" (Acts 3:6). Out of this
complete giving consciousness, the man was healed.

Kahlil Gibran, in his classic work *The Prophet,* says:

You give but little when you give of your posses-
    sions.
It is when you give of yourself that you truly
    give. . . .
Give as in yonder valley the myrtle breathes its
    fragrance into space.

"Bring the whole tithe into the storehouse" could imply
a commitment to work with the law in all aspects of life.
Prove me now, God is saying. Prove the law in action. This
involves going the second mile in meeting obligations,
turning the other cheek in relationships, and forgiving
until "seventy times seven." It means diligence in keeping
the high watch of positive thinking and loving reactions in

overcoming the world of tribulations. In other words, life is consciousness, so it is foolhardy to suppose that the law can be fulfilled by anything less than a total and broad commitment to achieving a high-level consciousness.

Jesus gave prime emphasis on giving as the way to achieve this degree of consciousness: give, and you will receive. Get the feeling of being a channel for the flow of good. Think give, and you will receive. Think of your work as giving. Think of every relationship as an opportunity to give. Give to your children. Give to your neighbors. Give to passersby on the street. Think give. Give way. Let!

And as part of this commitment to the giving consciousness, give of your substance, graciously, wisely, and without thought of return. Think not of what you are giving *to,* for that can turn the mind to condescension or giving *to be seen of men.* Rather think of what you are giving *from* and thus feel humble in realizing that you are simply giving way to the divine flow.

Certainly, a helpful and practical plan for getting order and system into your giving commitment is the way of tithing. It makes as much sense as keeping a budget, and it can be given an appropriate recognition in the budget. However, it is wise to remind yourself that the 10 percent is simply a disciplined reminder to bring the whole tithe. The giving consciousness must continue where the tithe check leaves off.

If one is sincere in the desire to grow and ultimately to put away childish things, a good plan is to use the tithing

slide rule as a means of checking up on your spontaneous giving during the year. In other words, instead of
following the regular ritual of writing a tithe check, work
for a commitment to give way to the divine flow on a sustained basis. Just let yourself be free, as a joyous giver with
no thought of contracts or bargains or great benefits of
success. Take pride in the growing maturity you demonstrate throughout the year by giving the whole tithe. And
then, at the end of the year, when you are engaged in an
audit of your fiscal year for tax purposes, total up your giving and see how close you actually come to a 10 percent
giving performance. What a tremendous feeling of fulfillment you will experience when you note that your giving
exceeded a tenth! Now it could be said you have put
away childish things, for the whole tithe now means *no
tithe*, in the sense of obligation. Now you are joyously in
the flow of life, through a giving consciousness. For a person is essentially a giving creature, and life is lived from
within out. On human levels of consciousness, one may
emphasize *getting* and *having* as the prime goals; in spiritual consciousness, one seeks the way of *giving* and *being*.

The crux of the statement in Malachi is "I will . . . open
you the windows of heaven, and pour you out a blessing."
This is usually quoted to indicate that if you tithe, everything in heaven and Earth will fall into your lap. But how
conveniently, in this instance, it is forgotten that heaven is
not "up there." Jesus clearly says that the kingdom of
heaven is within you. It is not a place in space but an

inner potentiality of *imprisoned splendor* that is released through you. Thus the windows of heaven are *in* you. The windows of heaven *are* you!

You are the windows of heaven, and you will be poured out as a blessing. And because you are in the flow of limitless substance by reason of your commitment to the whole tithe, the blessing that you *become* is more than sufficient to deal with any situation and to meet any and all requirements.

The emphasis is often upon the giving as returning to us from God "up there" or "out there" from the world. Let us not lose sight of the principle that God can do no more for us than God can do through us. The receiving is always a greater flow from within. It may be a flow of love or guidance or life or success-producing ideas, but the receiving is *in the same stream as the giving.*

The faucet is opened so that it can give, and the more it gives, the greater the flow by which to give. It may provide refreshment and the means of cleanliness for a household, but it is simply busy giving of itself. It may seem impractically idealistic to say that the purpose of giving is not to receive but to give. And yet, the moment we focus on receiving, we begin to lose the flow of giving. As Jesus said, "Do not let your left hand know what your right hand is doing" (Mt. 6:3). Otherwise, you could become like the Pharisee who sounded a bell as he gave so that everyone would know of his "great largesse." In the extreme, one might become as Eugene O'Neill says of his

Marco: "He is not even a mortal soul; he is only an acquisitive instinct." Give to give to give yet more. This is the
subtle and yet powerful meaning of the injunction: Think
give!

Let's hear less of tithing and more of giving. Let us not
be deluded by claims of "the magic law of tithing." Tithing is not a law but a technique for fulfilling the law of giving. There is no magic in it whatever, any more than
there is magic in the flow of water when the tap is turned
on. There is no need for magic when one works diligently
to keep in the flow of life.

Understand, this is not to say one should not give a
tenth or more of one's income. Tithing is a powerful technique to employ through which to achieve the discipline
of spontaneous giving. Ultimately you cannot really know
that you are a giver of the *whole tithe* until you test yourself by putting away the tithing practice for a period (even
one month is a good test) and still wind up with an equiva-
lent amount through spontaneous freewill giving. This
may be a challenge to some people who prefer to follow
the decimal way of giving. It is like a child learning to ride
a bike with training wheels and then continuing to use the
trainers throughout life. It is unlikely that he or she will
ever know if he or she could ride steadily without them.

Of course, it is vital that you get into a giving consciousness and let your hands give way to some kind of
giving flow. A disciplined program of tithing is certainly a
giant step in spiritual growth. We are simply suggesting

that you do not stop there. Dare to take the step beyond the tithing practice.

Will this mean less giving to churches and institutions? On the contrary, it should lead to a more sustained and generous outpouring, but from people who are released from the pressures and stringencies of decimal giving to the joy and affluence of true spiritual giving. In the end, worthy institutions should be more effectively supported and the givers should have increasingly a sense of fulfillment in knowing, at the end of each year, that their giving has actually achieved or exceeded the tithe. People who achieve this consciousness are truly ready to step forward into the new age.

CHAPTER **12**

A New World Vision

During the course of this book, we have been engaged in an extensive study of *spiritual economics*. Repeatedly, we have stressed the point that economic conditions, no matter how dire they appear to be, are in the world "out there." What counts for you is how you deal with them in consciousness. When you begin to see things from the high perspective of the ever-presence of God-substance, you will be in the creative flow of abundance, which will bless your life with sustained affluence. And it will also go forth from you as a prospering influence in the world.

This last statement may appear to be more poetry than realism. However, it is a fundamental of the prosperity law that is rarely addressed. Certainly every human heart longs for security and stability in financial affairs. But there is another side of this coin. One who achieves prosperity at once becomes an influence for abundance in the world. Jesus touched on this when he said, "I, when I am lifted up from the earth, will draw all men to myself" (Jn. 12:32). We will discuss this in greater detail later on in this chapter.

We all live and do business in the world, so it is not easy to maintain a high level of faith. In this time of mass communication, we are all exposed to a steady barrage of doom and gloom from forecasting economists, who use very convincing business statistics and "economic indicators." We would do well to listen to Paul: "Don't let the world around you squeeze you into its own mold, but let God remold your mind from within" (Rom. 12:2 Phillips).

It is important to impress yourself often with the great reassurance of the "unity principle," which we repeat here slightly paraphrased:

Wherever substance is at all, the whole of substance must be; and because substance is omnipresent, the whole of universal substance must be present at every point in space at the same time.

This is fundamental spiritual law. When you really know yourself as a spiritual being, you experience the fulfilling of the law, which "rushes, streams, and pours into you" in terms of substance and supply and all that is required for success. When Jesus said, "I came that they may have life, and have it abundantly" (Jn. 10:10), he was saying that the breakthrough he had made into Infinite Mind prepared the way for what Emerson called "an inlet that may become an outlet to all there is in God." It is in this consciousness that we can say, "Many times I have been broke, but I have never been poor." There may be times when you do not have sufficient money, but you can never be separated from the all-sufficiency of God-substance within.

Of course, not knowing this fundamental spiritual law, businesses do fail and people do go hungry. If you get caught up in the negativity of the times, read the gloomy stories of unemployment and business failures and watch the television documentaries dealing with mass starvation in other parts of the world, you could well react in fear and anxiety. One minister, borrowing the last three words of the classic movie *Bridge Over the River Kwai* announced as his sermon title, "Madness, Madness, Madness." The sermon was a negative forecast of world hunger and despair, pointing to the vague hope of an afterlife, and how in some far-off paradise things would be made right.

In orthodox Christian theology, the afterlife is a heaven of the skies where there are "golden streets" and presumably riches for all. It is almost beyond comprehension how this heaven "up there" became so rooted in the religious thinking of the Western world, especially since Jesus clearly located it: "The kingdom of God cometh not with observation . . . for, behold, the kingdom of God is within you" (Lk. 17:20–21 KJV).

Jesus was not talking about a place in space but a dimension of our minds, and he was saying that within every person there is limitless life, limitless substance, and open access to infinite intelligence. Lack of any kind in human experience is the result of some sort of obstruction in the free flow of the creative process. You cannot begin to understand the prosperity law until you are willing to accept this aspect, which means to take charge of your life. Your consciousness has, at the very least, contributed to putting you in the place where you happen to be. And the other side of this must also be true: when you begin to assume mastery over your thoughts, you become attuned to an evolution that leads to the unfoldment of the kind of things and experiences you desire.

The questions are frequently asked: "But is it possible for everyone to enjoy prosperity? Is there not a limit in the universe?" These are logical questions from a purely human perspective. In the field of economics, many of the modern-day "experts" have been influenced by the Malthusian doctrine propounded by the British economist Thomas Malthus in the eighteenth and early nineteenth centuries. He held that population always multiplies faster than its means of subsistence can be made to do. His gloomy prediction for the world of the future: poverty for everyone. Malthus was also a clergyman, but unfortunately he never made the discovery of the Allness and ever-presence of divine substance.

There is no question that we are facing a world in crisis. But let us look at the word *crisis* as the Chinese see it through the awkward process of translating it from English. They use the symbols for two words: *danger* and *opportunity.* Of course, we are facing critical times today and down the road into the future. However, we have the marvelous opportunity to usher in a new world in which people of awareness will live with what Thoreau calls "the license of a higher order of beings."

We will need to expose our children at a very early age in school to the idea of the spiritual universe and their own unique relationship to it. We are not referring to religion. Certainly we wouldn't want to see the education process confused by the infusion of chauvinistic theological points of view. However, there is a great need to help children to know themselves as whole persons in a whole universe. The very natural next step would be for high school and college students to be challenged with the concept of *spiritual economics.* Oliver Wendell Holmes once said, "A mind once stretched by a new idea can never go back to its original dimensions." When people have experienced expansions of their awareness of the prosperity principle, they will never be the same. Then they are ready to play a part in the new era as it unfolds.

There is now incontrovertible evidence that mankind has just entered upon the greatest period of change the world has ever known. The ills from which we are suffering have had their seat in the very foundation of human thought. But today something is happening to the whole structure of human consciousness. A fresh kind of life is starting. In the face of such an upheaval, actually shaken by it, no one can remain indifferent. Swept along by the tide of affairs, what can we do to see clearly and act decisively? No matter what reactions we may have to current events, we ought first to reaffirm a robust faith in the destiny of man.

—_Teilhard de Chardin_

While economists view the "world in crisis" with alarm, it is important that here and there new age thinkers like yourself hold to the vision of the spiritual human being who has always risen to the occasion to draw forth the wisdom and creativity required to take the next logical step in the progress of civilization. In other words, we are hopeful that you will achieve more from this study than just learning how to demonstrate the wherewithal to pay your bills. We want to see you plugged in to the universal process of growth, that you may become a vital part of the spiritualization of "the structure of human consciousness."

At Amherst College some years ago, a squash was

planted in good soil. When it had grown to about the size of a person's head, researchers put a band of steel around it with a harness attached to it so that they might discover the lifting power of the squash. They estimated that it might press five hundred pounds. In a month it reached a pressure of five hundred pounds. In two months it reached fifteen hundred pounds, then two thousand pounds, and they had to strengthen the bands. It finally reached the pressure of five thousand pounds when it broke the rinds. Upon opening the squash, the researchers were amazed to find it to be a mass of fibers that had developed in the attempt to fight away the obstacles that were hindering the growth of the squash. Further investigation revealed that eighty thousand feet of roots had grown, going out in all directions to find help and strength for the fibers which needed substance.

This experiment with the squash revealed that, due to the very nature of life, the crisis was the opportunity for new growth. It is almost as if, because it needed added power to break the bands, it mobilized every means available to accomplish it. We see this same process at work in nature's evolution. For instance, the giraffe developed a long neck because it needed it to reach the edible leaves of the tall trees that grew in its natural habitat. Birds developed their amazing homing instinct because they needed it to enable them to migrate from one part of the world to another and safely return "home." And when we face life with that "robust faith," we can know that we will develop the keys to peace and plenty, because we need them. An economic crisis, too, is the opportunity for growth.

Psychologists estimate that not one person in a million is living up to the best which is in him or her. Are you? Are you making the most of your inner resources? When you ride the subway or bus or stand in a crowded elevator, look into the faces of the people around you and try to imagine what life would be like if all these people should suddenly awake and become their best possible selves. Then, look in a mirror and reflect on this same thing. Can you imagine what your life would be like if you could realize your full potential?

This is not to discourage you in the awareness of how far we have to go. The important thing to know is that civilization is just beginning and the *best is yet to be*. The great wisdom of the ages still lies undiscovered in the depths of humanity's inner Self. The great capacity for health and eternal life still lies untapped within our life potential. The key to the kingdom of all-sufficiency, with work and food and abundance for all, still lies unused in the depths of our undeveloped faith. Of course, we are faced with very difficult personal as well as worldwide economic challenges, but we know that these are the best of times, for we have the opportunity to give birth to a new world.

In a book entitled *The Amazing Crusoes of Lonesome Lake*, Ralph Edwards tells of an interesting pioneering experience in the north woods of the Yukon. This family went there with nothing except their bare hands in an experiment to see if they could forge a life for themselves. The author comments, "In the beginning all we had was a lot of sheer necessity." In the same sense, the world's economic problems provide us with the sheer necessity, as Browning puts it, "to open out a way whence the imprisoned splendor may escape."

At this point, you might be wondering about the fact that Jesus said, "For you always have the poor with you" (Mt. 26:11). Doesn't this indicate that there will always be pockets of poverty in the world? Jesus, as was his wont, was speaking in a personally symbolic sense. The word *poor* as used here is from the root word that means "beggar." He was saying that we live in the world and absorb the limiting beggar thoughts by a process almost like osmosis. The challenge is to transcend the limitations and achieve a higher level of consciousness.

Unfortunately, society has accepted this dictum of having the poor always with us, which has given rise to the "welfare syndrome." Churches have long engaged in the work to feed and clothe the poor, which is commendable. But it is also a cop-out, for the church has done little or nothing to help the indigent ones to find their own *inlet which may become an outlet for all there is in God.* How great is the need to help people to know themselves as channels for the flow of God-substance from within, thus to help them to throw off the shackles of poverty and move up into the mainstream of affluent living.

As we look down the road into the future of civilization, it seems obvious that all religious institutions must set a high priority on the teaching of spiritual economics to their followers. People must not only engage in the practice of the presence of God, but they must also know that the kingdom of God, which is at hand, is a realm of substance that is omnipresent and omniactive. Religion must ultimately help all people to get into the creative flow of healing life, guiding intelligence, and limitless supportive substance.

A few years ago a man had a dream. He believed that economically deprived people could be spiritually rehabilitated and brought up into middle-class experience. With the cooperation of the New Jersey state unemployment and welfare agencies, he was given the names of five hundred chronic unemployables. These were people who had been unemployed for at least two years, during which time they had given up any hope of finding work and had settled into the support of the welfare system. These people were invited to enroll in a two-week crash course in building consciousness, changing their self-image, learning to think positively, learning how to focus their skills and write job resumes. Through the device of role playing, they learned how to apply for jobs, how to conduct themselves in interviews, and so on. Finally, at the end of the two weeks of concentrated training and already showing signs of new confidence, these people were turned out to seek employment on their own. They were given no leads nor help of any kind. In a sense, their tutors simply said, "Okay, now go out and find jobs." Within six months 80 percent of the group of five hundred people were gainfully employed. That means that four hundred people had actually been transformed from tax-exhausting welfare clients into tax-paying citizens. The report of this experiment included a careful follow-up of each person in the study. One can imagine this same program being put into operation on a nationwide basis, causing a rippling effect through every segment of society. What a tremendous impact it would have in lessening the welfare load and increasing the tax revenues! It could actually turn the nation's economy around in thirty days. The carefully documented report was called The Patterson Plan. You might wonder whatever became of it. Nothing!—which may well indicate that at least a part of the problem is the inertia of the whole welfare system, which is locked into the you-always-have-the-poor-with-you syndrome. The system was threatened by a plan that promised to relieve and possibly eliminate much poverty.

This very illumining research project clearly revealed that poverty is corrected, not by doling out money, but by helping people to change their self-image and achieve a "rich mentality." Charles Fillmore once said, "It is a sin to be poor." This is not judgmentally viewing the disadvantaged people of our society. The word *sin* to a student of metaphysics means "the frustration of potentiality." It is closely related to the Anglo-Saxon word *syne*, which was an archery term meaning missing the target. Thus sin is missing the mark of perfection, a block in the process of projecting one's potential divinity. Poverty as a collective condition can only be corrected by helping people, one by one, to *stir up the gift of God within them.*

This is not to say that the poor are responsible for the condition of poverty. But it is saying that every person must take charge of his or her own life. The experience of poverty in any life is the personal opportunity to awaken to a new consciousness and reveal a new order of life. People can begin with what they have and do what they can right where they are, even if all they really have is *a lot of sheer necessity.* But if they will affirm that "robust faith" in the Universe of order, they will experience a new consciousness that will guide their hands, direct their footsteps, and put words in their mouths in a great process of transformation from indigence to affluence.

The cynic will say, "You are dreaming! And anyway, there are no jobs to be had." At this point we desperately need the wisdom of Jesus, as he said, "Do not judge by appearances, but judge with right judgment" (Jn. 7:24). He also said, "I, when I am lifted up from the earth, will draw all men to myself" (Jn. 12:32). As one person changes his or her level of thought, the consciousness of the whole changes to that degree. As one person gets off welfare and begins even to gear his or her thinking toward productive work, there is a rippling effect through the entire economy of the nation, even of the world. True, the influence is small, certainly imperceptible, but it is real. It is much like the phenomenon described by astrophysicists: if one person waves a hand, he or she sets off a rippling effect in the atmosphere that has an effect on the farthest star. So as one or two persons here and there across the land begin to *think* work, *think* productivity, and *think* abundance, something happens. People become more secure and begin to purchase things; business begins to expand and thus takes on more workers; government pays out less in welfare and takes in more taxes, having the luxury of deciding whether to reduce taxes or to embark on new programs of social development; but in either case leading to economic health for the nation, which in turn becomes an affluence for prosperity for every person.

The exciting part of this cyclical process of prosperity in the world is that it has its genesis in the modest influence of two or three persons agreeing in a consciousness of prosperity and creativity. Just one person who changes his thoughts, becoming alive with the idea of the all-sufficiency of God-substance and staking his claim for prosperity and success in the world, not only begins to experience abundance in his own life, but also becomes a powerful influence for prosperity in the world. It is a total switch on the old cop-out that "when the economy improves, my situation will be better." It is the great new conviction that "when I move toward prosperity, the whole economy improves." Some Truth groups sing that powerful song by Sy Miller and Jill Jackson, *Let There Be*

Peace on Earth and Let It Begin With Me. Perhaps we should think in terms of blessing the economy of the world by singing, "let there be prosperity on Earth and let it begin with me." The words are not musically adaptable, but the idea can start a chain of power that will begin a definite move toward actualizing our new world vision.

Just think what this new concept means! The old theology taught, or at least strongly implied, that it is a sin to be prosperous. Thus there have often been subdued feelings of guilt associated with the desire for or the experience of abundance. In our new world vision, it is turned completely around. The righteous or right use of the laws of spiritual economics is a powerful influence for prosperity in the world. Of course, on the practical side, it means a great renaissance of self-reliance, where the individual does not look to others or to government for the means of her prosperity. She does what she can with what she has right where she is. She thus consciously becomes a receptive channel for the flow of God-substance. And in this person and those like her, we witness a hopeful return of the "self-made person."

Another recent significant study dealt with the problem of inflation. It fixed the major responsibility on productivity, and more specifically on worker attitudes. The report admitted that there could be no "quick fix," but that a start could be made by improving personal attitudes of every worker in the marketplace. We hear much about recessions and depressions as if we are referring to some great monster that has the world in its clutches. The fact is we have been in the midst of a *great depression of worker attitudes.*

In recent years there has been a spiralling upward sweep through industry and its workers of greater profits for inferior products and higher wages and less hours and less and less productivity in those hours. The time is ripe and "rotten ripe" for change. If there could be a mass turn-around in worker attitudes and productivity, with people caught up in the ideal of work as the opportunity to release their innate potential, there would be a great reversal of economic lows and inflationary trends in a matter of weeks.

Thus it can be seen that the solution to world economic problems is simple. It's not easy, but it is simple. Simple from the standpoint that it is not complex. It is not easy because it depends on people realizing that the heart of the problem is not "out there somewhere" but in the consciousness of each person. The sincere student of Truth will look in a mirror and say, "It is high time that you stopped being a part of the problem and became part of the solution." The solution is a collective consciousness of the ever-presence of God-substance. When you think abundance, even begin to experience the free flow of abundance in your life, you are a vital part of that which makes for prosperity for all.

Perhaps we should look back and see how we got to the present state of affairs. Our American forefathers were not unlike the followers of Moses in their flight from Egypt. Our people wandered in deserts far wider than

Sinai. We have built scores of cities grander than Jerusalem. We have erected hundreds of temples finer than Solomon's. And we have risen to a place of world prestige and power and affluence—and by right of consciousness, for that is the divine law. But we are seeing a change: much of our influence in the world is waning, our great cities are rotting from within, and our temples have lost their voices and their influence for good.

The Hebrew prophets spoke almost as one voice in proclaiming that prosperity and righteousness are closely linked—not the righteousness of the Pharisees who made a display of piety, but the "right use" of divine law in thought and in practice in the marketplace. To put it in the simplest terms, it means turning from a philosophy of "in gold we trust," back to the old-fashioned ideal of "in God we trust." The simple solution is to turn away from the contemporary trend of rampant materialism.

> "You have sown much, and harvested little; you eat, but you never have enough; you drink, but you never have your fill; you clothe yourselves, but no one is warm; and he who earns wages earns wages to put them into a bag with holes."
>
> *Haggai 1:6*

Doesn't this sound like a comment about today's high cost of living and the difficulty through inflation of keeping up with price increases? Actually, the words were uttered by

Haggai over 2500 years ago. He was talking about how to cope with a sick economy. How better could you describe inflation than carrying your wages in *a bag with holes.* Haggai's answer to the problem of the economy: "Go up to the hills and bring wood and build the house" (Hag. 1:8). In a personally symbolic sense, this says to go within in a time of silence and get a renewed awareness of God as your resource and then go about your business affairs in the strong consciousness of the omnipresence of substance.

As students of new consciousness thinking, we challenge you to take hold of this prosperity principle of the omnipresence of substance. Become a part of a new worldwide epidemic of faith in the conviction that there is no need for poverty or lack anywhere. Believe that you are always in the presence of limitless substance which you form and shape and release through your faith. Keep the high watch of Truth by knowing that, wherever you are and whatever your experience, you are an inlet and may become an outlet for the flow of God-substance. And remember, substance is not simply spendable money but that which gives value to everything you have, everything you do, everything you are. It is ideas; it is creativity; it is guidance; and it is health and vitality.

Listen to the words of Charles Fillmore as he sends out a clarion call to the new world vision:

In the new era now at its dawn, we shall have a spirit of prosperity. The principle of the Universal substance will be known and acted upon, and there will be no place for lack. Supply will be more equalized. There will not be millions of bushels of wheat stored in musty warehouses while people go hungry. There will be no over-production or under-consumption or other inequities of supply, for God's substance will be recognized and used by all people. Men will not pile up fortunes one day and lose them the next, for they will not fear the integrity of their neighbors. Is this an impractical utopia? The answer depends on you. Just as soon as you individually do your part in quickening the consciousness of the whole economy.

The great new world vision that Mr. Fillmore is talking about is now. "The kingdom of God is at hand." Wherever you may be, you are an unborn possibility of limitless life, limitless intelligence, limitless substance, and yours is the privilege and the responsibility of giving birth to it. If you are not demonstrating supply in an orderly and affluent way of life, you are frustrating your own potential. And you are also a part of the problem of society.

It is important for you, as a spiritual being, to experience wholeness in every area of life. You should be healthy, you should experience a life of love and fulfillment, and you should manifest harmony in all your affairs, leading to prosperity and success. But remember, the consciousness of society as a whole, which certainly includes your next-door neighbor, will be influenced for good or ill by the kind of thoughts that rule your mind and manifest in your world. So for the sake of humankind as a whole, as well as for your own experience, think substance, think prosperity, think plenty for all.

Of course, the world is so big and the problem of poverty and hunger so widespread that you may be thinking: But what can I do? How can I have any kind of influence on such a gigantic need? I am only one! Canon Farrar has the answer. Let him speak directly to you:

> I am only one, but I am one.
> I can't do everything, but I can do something.
> What I can do, I ought to do.
> And what I ought to do,
> By the grace of God I will do.

About the Author

Eric Butterworth is minister of Unity Center of Practical Christianity in New York City, where he has served for over 35 years. He conducts a program of public lectures, growth workshops, and retreats, and his radio broadcasts are heard in four states.

Ordained in 1948, he played a vital role in the organization of the present Association of Unity Churches. He has served churches in Kansas City, Pittsburgh, and Detroit and is considered to be one of the leading spokespersons and thinkers in both the Unity and New Thought movements.

He is a frequent contributor to *Unity Magazine.* Besides his many popular Unity cassettes, he has published numerous books with Unity including *In the Flow of Life, Unity: A Quest for Truth, Celebrate Yourself!, The Concentric Perspective,* and *MetaMorality: A Metaphysical Approach to the Ten Commandments.*

Mr. Butterworth was born in Canada and

raised in California. Since his mother was a Unity minister, he was raised with Unity beliefs. He says, "It seems natural to devote my life to the work of helping other people find the influence of Truth in their lives as I have known it in mine."

His wife Olga is an associate at the New York center.

Printed in the U.S.A.

186-2798-10M-3-01